Hands On, Thumbs Up

Other Books by Camilla Gryski

Cat's Cradle, Owl's Eyes: A Book of String Games
Many Stars and More String Games
Super String Games

Hands On, Thumbs Up

Secret Handshakes, Fingerprints,
Sign Languages,
and More Handy Ways to
Have Fun With Hands

Camilla Gryski

Illustrations by **Pat Cupples**

Addison-Wesley Publishing Company, Inc.

Reading, Massachusetts   Menlo Park, California   New York
Don Mills, Ontario   Wokingham, England   Amsterdam   Bonn
Sydney   Singapore   Tokyo   Madrid   San Juan
Paris   Seoul   Milan   Mexico City   Taipei

Many of the designations used by manufacturers and sellers to distinguish their products are claimed as trademarks. Where those designations appear in this book and Addison-Wesley was aware of a trademark claim, the designations have been printed in initial capital letters (i.e., Super Glue).

Library of Congress Cataloging-in-Publication Data
Gryski, Camilla.
    Hands on, thumbs up : secret handshakes, fingerprints, sign languages, and more handy ways to have fun with hands / Camilla Gryski ; illustrated by Pat Cupples.
        p.   cm.
    Includes bibliographical references and index.
    Summary: Explores the many aspects of the hands and what can be done with them, including finger tricks, special handshakes, and various kinds of sign language.
    ISBN 0-201-56756-3
    1. Hand—Juvenile literature.   [1. Hand.   2. Sign language.]
I. Cupples, Pat, ill.   II. Title.
QM548.G78   1991
611′.97—dc20   91-16204
                                                                          CIP
                                                                            AC

Hands On, Thumbs Up was originally published by Kids Can Press, Ltd., of Toronto, Ontario.

Edited by Valerie Wyatt
Design by N. R. Jackson
Set in 14-point Bodoni Book by Compeer Typographic Services Limited and Cypergraphics Inc.

1 2 3 4 5 6 7 8 9-AL-9594939291
First printing, July 1991

Addison-Wesley books are available at special discounts for bulk purchases by schools, institutions, and other organizations. For more information, please contact:

Special Markets Department
Addison-Wesley Publishing Company
Reading, MA 01867
(617) 944-3700 x 2431

Contents

THOUSANDS OF THANKS

I am grateful to the many experts who read, and often re-read, almost every word of this book. Thanks to Dr. Ken McCuaig, Department of Anatomy, University of Toronto, who read "Handworks" three times; to Lee Johnson, Educational Consultant, E.N.T. Clinic, Hospital For Sick Children, Sue Lanphier and Irene Kessel, who helped me understand sign language; to Don Hunka, Forensic Analyst, Ontario Provincial Police, who checked out my fingerprint section; to Kevin Seymour, Department of Vertebrate Paleontology, Royal Ontario Museum, for reading "Other Hands"; to Naomi Tyrrell, mime artist, for her help with the mime section; to William F. Sauter of the Myoelectric Department, Hugh MacMillan Rehabilitation Centre, for reading "High-Tech Hands"; to Charles Novogrodsky who looked over my version of baseball hand signals; to Dr. Fred Morgan, Professor of Physics, York University, and Stan Cuthand of the Saskatchewan Indian Cultural Centre who both added to "Handclaps"; to Jo Churcher, National Library Division, Braille Department, C.N.I.B., and to Joan Robinson who talked to me about Braille. Many thanks also to the people who unsuspectingly answered the phone when I called the Metropolitan Toronto Police, the Royal Canadian Mounted Police, the Construction Safety Association of Ontario, the Ontario Jockey Club, the Toronto Harbour Commissioners and the McLaughlin Planetarium. More thanks go to the library staff at the Royal Ontario Museum; Robarts Library, University of Toronto (especially Adrienne); the Metropolitan Toronto Reference Library; Boys and Girls House, the Osborne Collection of Early Children's Books and the Spaced Out Library of the Toronto Public Library; and Joan Nash of Edco, Newton North High School.

Kathryn Windham, Barbara Herd, Mary Anne Cree, Deborah Dunleavy, Caroline Parry, Linda Granfield and Damian Gryski contributed interesting bits of information and folklore.

Thank you Kids Can for letting me write what looked like nineteen books, and to a truly wonderful editor, Val Wyatt, who helped me shape it into one book.

Last thanks, and love, to Chester, Mark and Damian, who lived with me and "my book".

FOR DAMIAN,
who first read this book
over my shoulder.

". . . our hands,
what we have instead of wings,"

BRONWEN WALLACE
Learning From the Hands

HANDWORKS

Before I wrote this book, I didn't think much about hands—mine or anybody else's. I noticed if I scraped my knuckles or sprained my thumb, but the rest of the time I took my hands and all they could do for granted. Then I started to find out about hands. Everywhere I went, I saw people's hands: waving, clapping, dancing around in the air. Everybody I talked to had something to tell me about hands: a joke, a song, a trick, a game. When I began my research, I had lots of questions. The more I researched, the more questions I asked. Here are some of them. You'll find the answers in the book.

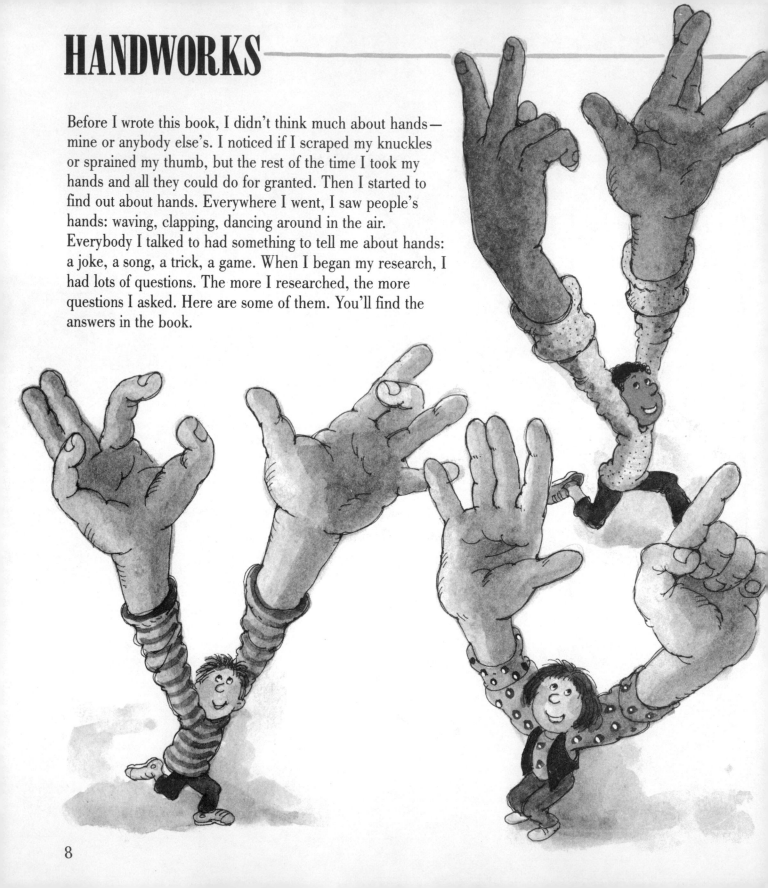

What is an opposable thumb? How does it help you hang on to things? (p. 22) Does anybody else have one? (p. 40)

How do you leave your unique signature on everything you touch?

WHAT'S IN A FINGERPRINT, ANYWAY? (P. 34) AND HOW CAN A FINGERPRINT BE A KEY? (p. 37)

How are your hands like the wings of bats . . . and the flippers of dolphins? (p. 43)

Why are left-handed pitchers called southpaws? (p. 49)

What does it mean when you win "hands down" or when you "wash your hands of something"? (p. 98)

How can your hand see in the dark and around corners? (p. 54) Can your fingertips see to read? (p. 56)

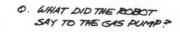

Q. WHAT DID THE ROBOT SAY TO THE GAS PUMP?

A. TAKE YOUR FINGER OUT OF YOUR EAR!

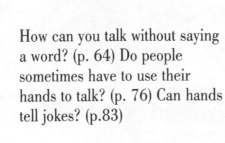

How can you talk without saying a word? (p. 64) Do people sometimes have to use their hands to talk? (p. 76) Can hands tell jokes? (p.83)

Have fun.

Camilla Gryski

9

Two amazing machines

Your hands are two amazing machines attached to the ends of your arms. Have you stopped and looked at them lately? Your hands work for you all day, every day. They hardly ever stay still, but they don't get tired unless you really overwork them. Your arms may ache, your feet may hurt, but did you ever hear anybody complain about tired hands?

Think about all the different things your hands do when you get home after school. You knock on the door or turn the doorknob to get into the house. The cat comes to greet you, so you bend down to give it a pat. On your way through the kitchen, you take the lid off the cookie jar and grab a couple of cookies. Your hand transports the cookies up to your mouth . . . delicious! You open the cupboard to get a glass—then you open the fridge and take out the milk. You pour the milk without spilling a drop. You turn on the TV or play a video game, thumb through a book or settle down to do some homework. You might go back outside to play a little basketball, climb a tree, skip, or ride your bike. Wherever you go and whatever you do, your hands are your helpers.

You hands are controlled by your brain. Your brain devotes lots of space to your hands. Homunculus is a picture of your body as "seen" by your brain. The hands are huge because it takes so many brain cells to move them around and figure out what information they're sending back. So if you knocked over a glass in the cupboard, or spilled the milk, it was your brain that was being clumsy!

10

PETER POINTER, TOBY TALL: SOME FACTS ABOUT FINGERS

When you were little, you sang lots of songs about Peter Pointer, Toby Tall and friends. But you probably didn't realize how important it is to give the fingers names instead of numbers. Is the First Finger the Index Finger or the Thumb? Is the Second Finger the Index Finger or the Middle Finger? Doctors especially must be clear about which finger they're describing.

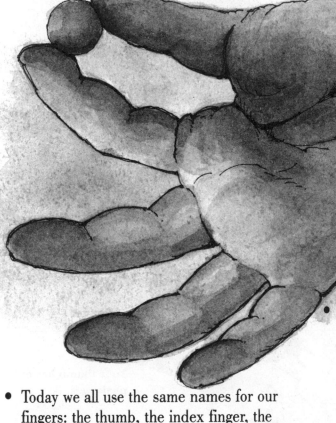

- Today we all use the same names for our fingers: the thumb, the index finger, the middle finger, the ring finger and the little finger.
- Some people call the little finger the pinkie. The name might come from the old Scottish word "pink," meaning little boat. The Dutch word for little finger is "pink," too.

- The old Latin names for the fingers told something about each one. The name for the little finger was Auricularis. The word auricular means having to do with the ear. The little finger is the best for scratching inside an itchy ear or cleaning out some wax.
- The ring finger was called Annularis. Annular means having to do with rings. The Romans believed that an artery ran from the heart to the fourth finger carrying love. Most people wear their wedding rings on this finger.

What's inside?

Your hands have been called powerful packages. Are you curious about what's inside? If you looked at your hands with X-ray eyes, here's what you'd see.

The bones of your fingers are called phalanges.

(One bone is called a phalanx.)

The phalanges meet at the joints of your fingers.

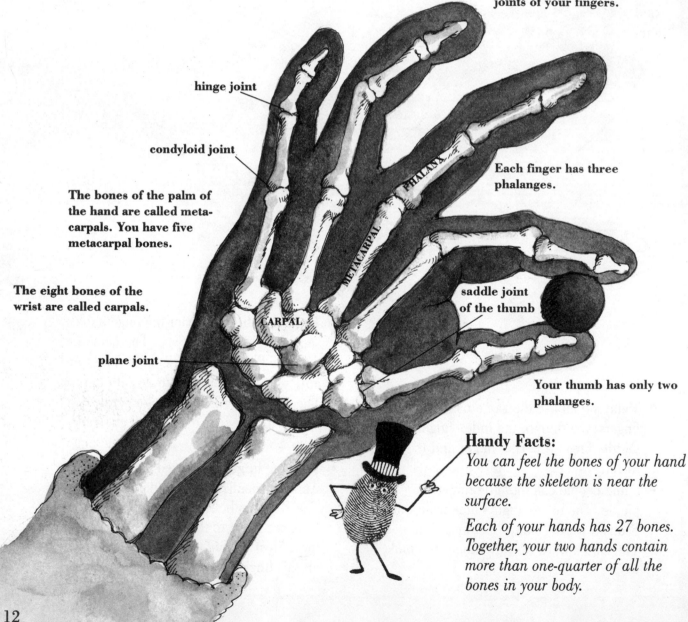

hinge joint

condyloid joint

The bones of the palm of the hand are called meta-carpals. You have five metacarpal bones.

The eight bones of the wrist are called carpals.

plane joint

PHALANX

METACARPAL

CARPAL

Each finger has three phalanges.

saddle joint of the thumb

Your thumb has only two phalanges.

Handy Facts:

You can feel the bones of your hand because the skeleton is near the surface.

Each of your hands has 27 bones. Together, your two hands contain more than one-quarter of all the bones in your body.

MOVE THOSE BONES

How does your hand move? The place where two bones meet is called a joint. Bones move at the joints. Inside each joint cavity, a slippery liquid called synovial fluid keeps the bones from rubbing against each other. The fluid doesn't drip out because each joint is inside a little bag or capsule. Cartilage—a kind of elastic tissue—coats the end of each bone and also stops the bones from rubbing together. The bones move easily. Easy movement cuts down on the body's wear and tear.

- You have rounded knuckles at the joints of your fingers.
- Bend and straighten your fingers to see the hinge joints move—like a door opening and closing.

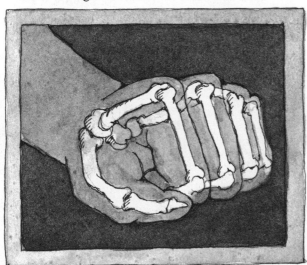

- Make a fist. Can you see the knuckles that are the ends of the metacarpal bones?
- The bones of the saddle joint of the thumb fit together like two saddles.

- Bend your fingers down like this to see the condyloid joints work like hinge joints. Condyloid joints also let you move each finger from side to side.

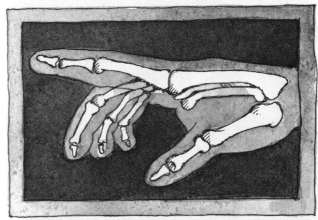

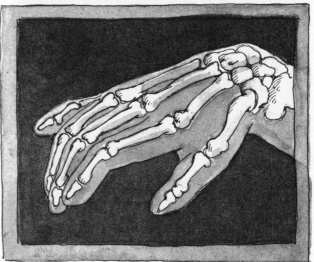

- Bend your hand down to see the bony arch of the carpal bones on the back of your wrist.

How many ways can you move your thumb? You can bend and straighten it and move it forwards and backwards. Your thumb can also rotate across your palm.

Teamwork

It takes teamwork to get your hand from your plate of toast to your glass of juice, and more teamwork to get the glass up to your mouth.

The hand has two assistants to move it around—your upper arm and your lower arm. Your hand can grasp things and let them go, but you need your arm to move them. If your shoulder or elbow is sore, you'll have trouble reaching for your juice.

Your arm gets your hand over to your glass of juice. Now how do you pick it up? You have to move those bones. The bones of your hand are moved by two sets of muscles working together—muscles in your hands and muscles in your forearms. The bulky muscles are in your forearms. They're outside of your hand so your fingers are slender enough for delicate movements.

Try making a tight fist, then opening out your hand. Can you see the muscles moving in your forearm? When you want to make a fist, your brain tells your muscles to contract. The muscles contract and they pull on the bones, then they relax until they're needed again.

The muscles that help you flex (bend) your hand and fingers are called flexors. They are on the front of your lower arm. You watched the flexors move when you made a tight fist.

The muscles that help you extend (straighten out) your hand and fingers are called extensors. They're on the back of your lower arm. Open your hand and stretch it out to see the extensor muscles at work.

There are also small muscles in your hand itself. They work with the muscles of the lower arm and help you move your fingers and thumb from side to side.

What carries the muscle power from your lower arm to your fingers so they can grab that glass of juice? Long strong cords called tendons run from the muscles in your lower arms to your hands. They cross the joints and are anchored to the bones of your fingers. The muscles are the pullers or puppeteers and the fingers are the puppets. The tendons are the puppet strings.

You can see tendons move on the back of your hand when you tap your fingers on a table, or pretend to play the piano in the air.

Bend your index finger. Straighten it out. Now move it to one side, then to the other. For each of those movements, there is a tendon-muscle team. If a joint can move in four different directions, there must be four tendon-muscle teams.

So next time you're thirsty, think about all the bones, muscles and tendons that work together so you can take a sip of juice.

WRIST RESEARCH

Wiggle your fingers and move your wrist at the same time. It feels funny, doesn't it? When your wrist is moving, your fingers are usually still or hanging onto something. And when your fingers are moving, your wrist isn't. That's because the long muscles controlling the fingers work best when the wrist is still.

When your wrist is bent forwards as far as it will go, your hand's grip is weak—only a quarter of its usual strength. For a strong grip, make a tight fist with your hand. Now look at your wrist. It's not perfectly straight. Your hand naturally bends back a little.

ARM MOVES

Try this nifty trick to see how your arms move your hands around.

1. Stand with your arms by your sides. Your hands are facing palms forward.

2. Raise your arms out to the side.

3. Bring your arms forward, until they are sticking straight out in front of you. What's happened to your hands? Are the palms facing each other now?

4. Let your arms drop to your sides.

Look at your hands. When you began, the palms were facing out; now the palms are touching the sides of your legs. You didn't twist them. All the movement happened in the shoulder joint.

Here's another way your arm moves your hand.

1. Put your hand out in front of you, palm down. Now rotate it until the palm is facing up. This movement is called supination. If you were going to eat or "sup" out of your hand, you'd hold it like this.

2. Rotate your hand until the palm is facing down again. This is called pronation. Prone means "face down."

The palm-up, palm-down movement is all in your forearm, not in your hand. Next time you drink a glass of juice, watch what happens to your forearm as the level of liquid goes down. Is the movement pronation or supination?

MUSCLE MEANING

The word "muscle" comes from the Latin word for mouse (*mus*), because some muscles are shaped like little mice.

16

JAN
FEB
MARCH
APRIL
MAY
JUNE
JULY

THE KNUCKLE CALENDAR

You can use your knuckles to help you remember which months of the year have 31 days and which don't.

Make your hand into a fist. Start counting with the knuckle of your index finger. It's January and January has 31 days. All the knuckle months have 31 days. February is the hollow between the knuckle of your index finger and the knuckle of your middle finger. Hollow months don't have 31 days. March is the knuckle of your middle finger. You know how many days knuckle months have.

When you run out of knuckles, start again with your index finger. August is a knuckle month, September isn't. Keep going to figure out the rest of the year yourself.

A BUILT-IN CUP

You have a handy cup that you take with you wherever you go. It never has to go into the dishwasher, but you wash it every time you take a bath or shower. It's most useful when you're outdoors and want to take a drink from a fresh natural spring. You make this drinking vessel when you "cup" your hand. The walls of this cup are made by your fingers, your thumb and the muscles at the base of your thumb, and a mysterious little muscle called the palmaris brevis.

The palmaris brevis makes a ridge on the little finger side of your palm. Most muscles are attached to bones, but the palmaris brevis is a surface muscle that's attached to skin instead of bones. It's a bit like the muscles horses use to ripple their skin when pesky flies bother them.

This built-in cup is called the cup of Diogenes, after a Greek philosopher. Diogenes lived a very simple life with few possessions like cups and dishes.

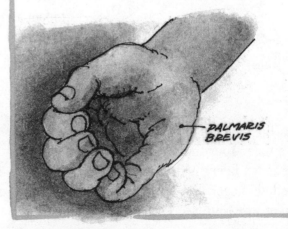

PALMARIS BREVIS

Finger tricks . . .

Rest your fingertips and thumb lightly on a table. Lift them up off the table, one at a time. Do some fingers move more easily than others?

Your index finger has lots of lift. That's because it has an extra extensor tendon that lets it move independently of the other fingers. The middle finger has some lift too, though not as much as the index finger. The poor old ring finger can barely lift itself off the table. That's because its extensor tendon is tethered (tied) to the tendon that goes to the middle finger. The ring finger has more lift when you lift up the middle finger at the same time. The little finger has an extra extensor tendon too, so it can lift itself high up off the table.

Try some tricks to find out more about how your fingers work.

The Tendon Trick

Here's a way to show what happens when the middle finger and the ring finger don't work together.

1. Put your hand on the table again. Your fingertips and thumb should rest lightly on the surface.

2. Bend your middle finger at the middle joint, and tuck it underneath your hand as shown.

3. Try to lift up your fingers one at a time. Your thumb is okay, the index finger is fine and so is the little finger. But the ring finger won't budge. That's because the ring finger and the middle finger are doing opposite things. The middle finger is bent, or flexed. The ring finger is straight or extended. Remember that the ring finger tendon is tied to the middle finger tendon. The middle finger tendon is holding the ring finger tendon in a flexed or bent position so you can't extend the ring finger.

People who play the piano do finger exercises on the piano to train all their fingers to move more independently. So don't try to fool a pianist with the Tendon Trick. She might be able to lift her trained ring finger up off the table!

Sweethearts

You can use both hands in this position to tell the story of two sweethearts.

1. Put your hands together, fingertips touching.

2. Bend your middle fingers down and press them against each other.

3. Now you can tell the story. You can separate the mother and the father—your thumbs. You can separate the brother and the sister—your index fingers. You can separate the aunt and the uncle—your little fingers. But you can't separate the sweethearts—your ring fingers.

The Wimpy Fingertip

Here's a funny trick to play on a friend. It works because of the tethered tendons of the middle and ring fingers. Tell your friend you can make one of her fingertips go all floppy, no matter how hard she tries to keep it straight.

1. Ask her to put her hand out towards you, palm up.

2. Now tell her to bend her ring finger in towards the palm of her hand. She must keep all her other fingers straight.

3. Now flip the tip of her ring finger up and down. No matter how hard she tries, she won't be able to keep the fingertip still.

Because the middle finger is extended, and the tendons of the middle finger and the ring finger are tied together, the muscle that controls the tip of the ring finger can't do its job very well. Try it on yourself. It feels (and looks) weird.

...AND DIGITAL DECEPTIONS

How many fingers do you have? Here's a way to prove you have eleven!

1. Count the fingers on one hand, but start at ten and count backwards. If you're using your right hand to count the fingers on your left, your thumb is 10.

2. Continue counting backwards to your little finger: 9 – 8 – 7 – 6. So far you have six fingers.

3. You have another five fingers on your right hand, so that's 6 plus 5. 6 + 5 = 11. You have eleven fingers!

Here's a way to lose a finger.

1. Interlace your fingers. Make sure your left thumb is on top.

2. Tuck your right middle finger inside your hands. Two fingers of your left hand are side by side.

3. Move your ring finger over to fill in the space where your middle finger used to be.

4. To make the interlace right, just change the way your little fingers cross over. When a friend counts your fingers, there are only nine!

Handy facts, handy fun

The Hand of Glory

A severed hand was a grisly part of a burglar's kit about 200 years ago. If the hand was taken from the right person—a hanged man was best—and prepared in the right way—preserved with saltpetre, salt and pepper, then dried in the sun—it was said to have magical powers. People believed this Hand of Glory could open locks and make thieves invisible.

When the burglar lit a candle the hand was holding (or lit the fingers and thumb of the hand itself), all the people in the house were supposed to fall into a deeper sleep. If the thumb refused to catch fire, then someone in the house was awake.

The story says the flames on a Hand of Glory couldn't be blown out, or put out with water, lemonade or anything else you can think of—except milk, which has power over evil spells.

In 1831, some burglars tried to break into a house in County Meath, Ireland. They brought a Hand of Glory with them, hoping that the magic would work. But everyone in the house woke up, and the burglars ran away, leaving their Hand of Glory behind.

RINGS ON YOUR FINGERS

Q. What has neither top nor bottom, but can hold flesh, blood and bone?

A. *A ring.*

A legend says that the first ring was worn by Prometheus, who stole fire from the gods to give to people. As a punishment, he was chained to a rock on Mount Caucasus. His chains were broken after 30 years of suffering, but he had to wear a link on one finger. The link had a piece of the rock set into it, so Prometheus was never really free.

There's something magical about a circle that has no beginning or end. Maybe that's why rings have been called magic circlets and were thought to have special powers.

When Mozart was 14 years old, he played the harpsichord in public in Naples. He played so well that the audience thought he was wearing a magic ring, and they demanded that he take it off his finger.

All Wound Up!

Tie yourself up in knots with this trick.

1. Put your arms straight out in front of you, the backs facing each other and the palms facing out.

2. Cross one arm over the other so that the palms are facing each other. Interlace your fingers and hang on.

3. Bend your elbows out and twist your hands until they're facing up. Your fingers should be close to your nose.

4. Straighten up your index fingers. The back of the index finger facing towards the left touches the left side of your nose. The back of the index finger facing towards the right touches the right side of your nose.

5. Now try to unwind your fingers, starting with your little fingers. If the trick works, all your fingers unwind, and you end up with your left index finger touching the left side of your nose, and your right index finger touching the right side of your nose.

6. Smile and waggle all your fingers.

Did you get stuck? Here's the secret. If you cross your right arm over your left, your right little finger must be on top when you interlace them. If you start by crossing your left arm over your right, your left little finger must be on top.

Now try it on a friend, and see what happens!

Thumbs up

Look at your thumb. It's shorter and fatter than your other fingers, and it sticks out by itself. Scientists say your thumb is opposable. This means it can swing around to face the palm of your hand, so that its pad can touch the pads of the other fingers. The others fingers—especially the index and middle fingers—have to help by bending and rotating a little to meet the thumb pad to pad.

Your hands are more skilful than the hands of any other creature. They can hang on to things

Q. WHY CAN'T AN ELEPHANT RIDE A BICYCLE?

A. HE DOESN'T HAVE A THUMB TO RING THE BELL!

PUP

PET

with a strong powerful grip, or they can hold small objects delicately between the tips of thumb and fingers.

Your thumb is your most important and busiest digit. It does almost half of the work of your hand. If you don't believe it, try living without your thumb for a little while. Tape your thumbs firmly to the sides of your hands so you can't use them—and you'll soon see how much you need them. You might even need help to tape that second thumb down! Try doing up the zipper on your jacket, taking the top off the strawberry jam, writing your name, or catching a ball.

HANDY MAN

Two million years ago, an early human called Homo habilis or "handy man" had hands that looked a lot like yours. Early humans made and used stone tools and carried food from place to place. Some scientists think that when people were able to handle things, they could name them, and that's how language developed.

What happens if someone is born without a thumb, or loses a thumb through injury? Today, doctors can do a lot to give someone a working thumb. It's possible to move another finger (often the index finger) into the thumb position to make a new thumb. A hand with three fingers and a thumb may look strange to you, but the way it works is more important than the way it looks. A big toe or second toe can also become a thumb.

If a new thumb can grip strongly, can be opposed to one or two fingers and has some feeling or sensation, it can take its place as the hand's most important digit.

THE FAR SIDE   By GARY LARSON

"Well, there it goes again . . . And we just sit here without opposable thumbs."

Thumblings

Thumbelina and Tom Thumb were little people, only the size of a thumb, who never grew any bigger. Because they were so small, they had marvellous adventures, some delightful and some terrifying.

Thumbelina made friends with a butterfly who pulled her along on her water-lily leaf, but then she was snatched and carried away by a cockchafer (stag-beetle).

Tom Thumb was a rogue who sneaked into his friend's pockets to steal their supplies of cherry

stones or pins when they were playing games. He was also boiled in a pudding and swallowed in turn by a cow, a giant and a fish.

France has "Le petit Poucet" (Hop o' my Thumb) who was no bigger than a thumb when he was born. And a little person only a finger and a half tall—with hair three fingers long—appears in Bengali fairy tales.

Where did these little thumblings come from? Some people think they came from a Hindu belief that the soul or innermost self, the size of a thumb, lived in the heart of each person. These thumb-sized souls danced inside the heart, stamping out the heartbeat.

No human beings are as small as thumblings, but Charles Stratton was a lot smaller than most people. General Tom Thumb, as he was called, was born in Bridgeport, Connecticut, in 1838. His parents were of normal size, but Charles stopped growing at six months. In his teens, Charles weighed only 7 kg (15 pounds) and stood 64 cm (25 inches) tall. Later on, he weighed 32 kg (70 pounds) and grew to 102 cm (40 inches tall). P.T. Barnum took him to France and to England, where he delighted the royal family by using his cane to fence with Queen Victoria's favourite poodle.

In 1863 he married the diminutive Lavinia Warren, who weighed just 13 kg (29 pounds) and was only 81 cm (32 inches) tall. Their lavish wedding ceremony was attended by nearly a thousand guests.

Measure up

Does your face measure up? It should—if you use your thumb. How big is your ear? Use your thumb as your tape measure. Your ear is the same size as your thumb, right?

What's the distance between your chin and the tip of your nose? Surprise! The same as your thumb.

Keep moving up your face. Measure from the tip of your nose up to your eyebrows. Now measure from your eyebrows to your hairline. Funny thing, your thumb fits there too. How about the distance between the outer corner of your eye and your ear? Your thumb again. Measure the distance from the middle of your face (between your eyebrows) to the outer corner of your eye. You know the answer this time.

Pouce is the French word for thumb. A *pouce* measures about an inch. Other parts of your hand can be used as rulers, too. A digit is the width of a finger—about 2 cm (¾ of an inch). The hand or handbreadth is the width of a hand across the palm—about 10 cm (four inches). It's used for measuring the height of horses.

STAMPING GREY MULES

There may not be too many grey mules where you live, but if you see one, here's what you do to get good luck.

When you see the mule, you lick your thumb. Then you twist the wet thumb back and forth in the palm of your other hand. Finish off by stamping that palm—hitting it with the side of your fist.

This superstition comes from Alabama, where they have grey mules. If you can't find a grey mule, try it with a grey horse!

Nailed you!

Every day your hands go out into the world to do battle. They are right out there on the front lines, grasping, poking, getting scraped and banged. Fortunately, your sensitive fingertips have some protection. When they go into battle, they carry shields—your fingernails.

Fingernails probably started out as claws. Over millions of years, they flattened and spread out over the fingertip. Fingernails are made of keratin, a kind of protein, and so are horns and hair. Some scientists think nails evolved from scales, the kind that covered the bodies of early reptiles, but stopped before they turned into hair. We're lucky they did.

Nails protect your fingertips and give the pads of your fingers a stiff backing. So they help you pick up things. Here's how. The fleshy tips of your fingers are much wider than the bones inside. Without the nails, the skin of your fingertip would just slip over the thin bone, and your fingers would slide right off what you want to pick up.

Your nails have also been called a built-in tool kit. They're good for scratching an itch and opening all kinds of packages. And because they're flat, not long and curved like claws, they don't get in the way when you try to pick things up.

Nails grow from the nail organs at the roots of the fingernails. You can't see them, because they're buried under the cuticle at the base of your nail. Nails never rest. They grow all the time. But they grow faster in summer than in winter. The thumb nail grows the fastest, and the little finger nail is the slowest. If you're a leftie, the fingernails on your left hand will grow faster than the nails on your right hand. If the right hand is your dominant hand, its nails will grow faster. And if you bite your nails, they'll grow faster, even though they never seem to get any longer.

It's easier to see the lunula—or little half-moon —on the nails of your thumbs and index fingers. The bigger the lunula, the faster the nail is growing. The lunula is white because the skin layer underneath it is thicker, and the pink blood vessels of the nail bed can't show through.

The condition of your nails can tell a doctor how healthy you are. A severe illness such as pneumonia can interrupt the nail growth and leave grooves in the nails, called Beau's lines. Brittle nails that split or break easily, thin eggshell nails or bitten nails tell the doctor something about her patient.

Your nails grow about .1 mm (.004 inch) a day —that's a lot more slowly than your hair. It takes about three months for a whole new nail to grow. If you didn't cut or bite your nails, they would start to twist as they grew, like the horns of a ram.

In China, very wealthy people used to let some or all of their fingernails grow as long as possible to show that they didn't have to do any work with their hands. To protect these long nails, they wore silver or gold sheaths or nail covers. Tz'u-hsi, the Empress Dowager of China until she died in 1908, wore guards of jade or gold set with rubies and pearls to protect the 15-cm (six-inch) long nails on her ring and little fingers.

YOUR FORTUNE IN YOUR NAILS

The little white spots in the keratin of your nail may show where you banged it. Some people think you can count the spots and find out all sorts of interesting things.

- Each spot is a present or a letter you will receive. It should arrive at your door when the spot grows to the tip of the nail where it can be cut.

- If you count the spots just before Christmas day, they'll tell you how many gifts you'll get.

- The number of spots will tell you whether you have a friend, a foe, some money or a beau (a boyfriend or girlfriend).

NAIL ART

Long ago, women in Egypt used to dye their fingernails red with henna. People still paint their nails with nail polish. Some artists are using acrylic paints and airbrush techniques to create fingernail art—everything from colourful patterns to flowers and tigers. If you could paint anything you liked on your fingernails, how would you decorate them?

THUMB-BELLS AND FINGER HATS

Do you have a thumb-bell at your house, or perhaps a finger hat to protect your sensitive fingertips? The place to check is a sewing kit.

Thumb-bell, thymelle, thimbell are all old names for the sewing tool you call a thimble. Finger hat is a translation of the German name *Fingerhut*.

Thimbles protect the sensitive fingertip that has to keep pushing the needle through material. Tailors, shoemakers and embroiderers all need shields for their fingers.

Some people think there have been thimbles as long as people have been sewing. We know there were thimbles as early as 79 A.D. Bronze thimbles were buried by the eruption of Mount Vesuvius and were found at Herculaneum and Pompeii.

The first thimbles were probably made of stone or bone. Later ones were made of bronze, then silver and gold, with precious stones like diamonds and rubies. These fancy thimbles were probably gifts that were treasured, but not used. Sometimes thimbles had romantic messages or carried reminders like "Remember me."

You don't need to sew to use thimbles. Put them on your fingers and scrape them up and down a metal washboard to play some great homemade music.

CUT 'EM!

Here's an old nursery rhyme that tells you when to cut your fingernails.

Cut them on Monday,
You cut them for health;
Cut them on Tuesday,
You cut them for wealth.
Cut them on Wednesday,
You cut them for news;
Cut them on Thursday,
A new pair of shoes;
Cut them on Friday,
You cut them for sorrow;
Cut them on Saturday,
See your true love tomorrow.

Did you notice Sunday's missing? Well, don't ever cut your nails on Sunday. Here's how the rhyme ends.

Cut them on Sunday, cut them for evil,
For all the next week you'll be ruled by the devil.

Another version says:
For all the next week you'll be cross as the devil.

29

All wrapped up

What's stretchy, tough and sensitive and works like the tires on your car? It's the stuff that wraps up the packages of your hands—your skin. You may say that you know something like you know the back of your hand, but maybe you don't know the back of your hand (or the palm) as well as you think.

The skin on the back of your hand is loose and elastic. When you pinch up a bit of it and let it go, it springs back right away. Well, right away if you're young. The older you get, the longer it will take to flatten out.

Your knuckles look like elephant's knees. The skin is loose and baggy. It has to be so that your fingers can bend. Your skin fits comfortably on your fingers, more like old jeans with baggy knees than new tight ones.

Try this to see how much your skin stretches when you bend your fingers.

1. Cut a strip of paper to be your skin ruler.

2. Attach your skin ruler to your wrist with tape. Put the tape on the paper first, then stick it to your wrist. You can make a little dot with a pen to be your starting point.

3. Make a fist and bend the paper around your knuckles. Put a mark on the paper where it reaches the tip of your middle finger.

4. Straighten out your fingers. Make another mark on the skin ruler at the tip of your middle finger.

Trim the paper at the first mark you made to see the distance from your wrist to your fingertip when you make a fist. Cut it again at the second mark. The piece you cut off shows you how much your skin stretched.

Q. WHAT KIND OF TREES DO YOU FIND ON YOUR HAND?

A. PALM TREES OF COURSE!

The stretchy skin on the back of your hand has some hair. If your hands aren't hairy, find some that are. Here's what you'll discover. There's hair on the back of the hand and the backs of the fingers, except for the ends of the fingers, which are bare. The knuckles are bare too. All the hair grows towards the little fingers.

richest supplies of sweat glands. As many as 340 may be jammed into a space this small. Sweat glands are handy to have. Damp skin holds on better than hard dry skin, and it's more sensitive. Did you ever notice how you lick your finger to lift up the corner of a page or how workers spit in the palms of their hands to get a better grip on their tools?

Look at the palm of your hand again and the fronts of your fingers. Can you see all the lines? Some are called flexure lines. They are the skin creases that follow the movements of the joints. The lines are where the joints bend.

This works fine for the end joints of your fingers, and for the second joints of your fingers. But when you get to the lines at the base of your fingers — watch out. They're right in the middle of a bone. No joint there!

Most people have two creases that run almost all the way across their palms. There's a line that shows how the thumb moves, and another line that runs up the middle of your palm. Watch the way your skin folds when you start to close your fingers into a fist — along the creases!

The other lines on the palm of your hand are tension lines (they show where the skin stretches) and papillary ridges. Papillary ridges help you pick things up or hang onto something tightly. The lines give you a good grip, just the way the treads on a car's tires give it traction on slippery streets. Try this test to see what happens when your fingertip treads can't hang on. Put some sticky tape over the tips of your index fingers and thumbs. Now try to pick up a piece of paper, or a dime — or turn a page of this book. Would you rather have smooth fingertips or ones with ridges?

Now turn your hand over, and look at the palm. Unless you're a werewolf, there's no hair there. The skin is thicker than the skin on the back of your hand, and it's firmly attached. You can't move it the way you can move the skin on the back of your hand.

The palms of your hands have one of the body's

The palm forecast

Palmistry is the art of telling a person's character and future by looking at the lines and shapes of the palm. Palmists call these lines the Heart Line, the Head Line, the Life Line and the Fate Line.

Here's a story from the Ivory Coast in Africa that explains why we have lines on the palms of our hands.

An old, old lady lived with her grandsons beside a lagoon. She left them food every day when she went to work in the fields. Her small share she put in a little crock on a high shelf to eat when she returned home.

But there came a time when her food began to disappear. At first, she thought that the mice and rats had discovered where she hid her food, so she put the crock on a different shelf. But the next evening there were only two mouthfuls left at the bottom of the crock.

Each day, she changed the hiding place. She put a cover on the crock. Then a stone on top of the cover. The mysterious thief just moved the stone and took off the cover. Finally she put the food inside the crock, put on the cover, turned a big gourd upside down over the crock and put the

gourd inside a heavy pottery jar. That evening, there were only a few crumbs left, and the old woman went to bed hungry again.

The next morning she asked each grandson one question.

"Which one of you has been taking my food and eating it?"

Nobody would admit to being the thief.

The old woman took them down to the water. "The spirit of the lagoon will tell me who is the guilty one."

One by one, the grandsons went towards the water singing. "If it was me who stole the food, water take me into your depths."

The water stayed calm and smooth until it was the turn of the last grandson. Legs shaking, teeth chattering, he began to sing. As he stammered the words, the water began to boil up, and the surface of the lagoon was covered with waves and zigzag lines. The water rose to his knees, to his thighs, to his navel, until he sank beneath the surface.

Now the grandmother bitterly regretted losing her temper and threw herself into the lagoon to save her grandson, but the child sank so quickly that she could only grab his hair. Again and again the wet hairs slipped through her fingers until finally she caught them and held them tightly. She made the spirit of the lagoon give back the child.

But the hairs had left fine marks on the palms of the grandmother's hands — lines straight and curved. And since that time, the palms of our hands have been criss-crossed with lines. If that child hadn't lied, the palms of our hands would still be flat and smooth, like those of our ancestors.

MONEY ITCHES

If your palm itches, you'd better pay attention. If it's the palm of your right hand, you'll receive some money. But if your left palm itches, you have to pay some money out.

BETRAYED BY HER HANDS!

An old story shows that it's not always good to have soft, lily-white skin on your hands.

Mary Queen of Scots was being held prisoner in the castle of Lochleven. She tried to escape by boat, disguised as a launderess carrying a bundle of clothes. Her face was covered up, and one of the men who was rowing the boat said jokingly, "Let us see what manner of dame this is." He tried to pull down the muffler that covered her face. When she put up her hands to stop him, the boatmen could see how fair and white they were — not a bit like the red, chapped hands of a launderess.

The story says that Mary begged them to row her to the shore, but they paid no attention to her. Instead, they rowed her back to her castle prison.

The fingerprint file

You're the detective at the scene of a burglary. If you're lucky, your burglar was very nervous and touched everything. Here's why you're lucky and the burglar isn't.

Fingerprints are the marks left by the ridges on your fingers. Along the tops of these ridges are the openings for the sweat glands in your fingers. So when you touch something, you leave behind a sweat print, plus oil that your fingers pick up from other parts of your body, like the skin on your nose.

What's in a fingerprint? Water, salt, fat, oil, amino acids and other chemicals. The more nervous the burglar, the more he sweats, and the more of everything he leaves behind for you to find. If he touches a smooth, flat surface, you might be able to see his prints. Look at a glass you've picked up. You leave visible prints—prints you can see.

Most fingerprints are hidden; they're called latent prints. First you have to look for them, then make them visible. There are different ways of developing prints so you can see them.

If you're looking for prints at the scene of the crime, you might use fingerprint powder. The powder sticks to the moisture and oils in a fingerprint. You dust surfaces with the powder to make the prints show up. Then you brush off the extra powder very gently so you don't disturb the print. Dusting works best on recent prints and surfaces that are non-porous (don't soak up the moisture).

Some chemicals can make prints visible, too. They react with some of the things in sweat—like amino acids or salt—to make them change colour so you can see them. Chemicals work well on porous surfaces such as paper and cardboard.

Two officers in a police department in Northamptonshire, England, discovered that Super Glue fumes work on fingerprints too. They used Super Glue to repair a tank in their darkroom. When they came back to check on the repair, they could see white powdery fingerprints on the tank. The fumes from the glue had reacted with the residues left by their fingers to make their fingerprints visible. Today, police have special kits to develop fingerprints this way. The kits contain the chemicals used in instant-bonding glues and other chemicals that help speed up the process.

Police also use laser light to look for fingerprints. Because laser light doesn't damage or change an object, it's often the first method the police use.

The laser makes the fingerprint fluoresce (it glows). Lasers can find fingerprints on porous materials like fabric and leather. One laser even found fingerprints on a postcard. The fingerprints were 40 years old!

Once you've found a fingerprint—or maybe several—what do you do next? You can't carry around a wall or a car window, but you can photograph the fingerprint on it, or use sticky tape to "lift" the fingerprint off the surface.

Here's how to lift your fingerprint right off your finger so you can look at it.

1. Use a pencil to make a black smudgy patch on a piece of paper.

2. Rub your finger across the patch until it's black to

3. Stick a piece of clear tape over your black fingertip. Give it a rub to make sure it's well stuck.

4. Lift the tape off your finger and the black fingerprint comes too. Stick the tape onto a piece of white paper and label it with the name of the finger and the hand.

Look at your fingerprint. You are looking at a one-of-a-kind. There are billions of fingerprints in the world, but no two are alike. Even identical twins have different fingerprints. You have your fingerprints five months before you are born. You can't get rid of them, and they will never change.

People have known for thousands of years that each fingerprint is unique. The Babylonians pressed fingerprints into clay to identify the authors of cunieform writings. In the third century B.C., Chinese businessmen put their fingerprints on the wax that sealed important documents. Most museums have fingerprints left by accident on ancient clay pots.

The fingerprint on your piece of tape is one of three general patterns. It's an arch, a loop or a whorl.

March with the arches

The lines in arches flow across your fingertips from one side to the other with an arch in the middle. That's a plain arch. A tented arch has a tent shape that sticks up in the middle. There aren't too many arches around.

The loop group

Loops that flow towards your little finger are called ulnar loops. Loops that flow towards your thumb are called radial loops. Loops are the most common fingerprint pattern. There are more ulnar loops than radial loops.

Whirl with the whorls

Plain whorls have spirals, ovals or circles in the centre.

There are three other kinds of whorls—the central pocket loop, the double loop and the accidental whorl.

The central pocket loop is just what it says—the ridges flow across your finger like a loop, but there's a little whorl in the centre.

The accidental whorl is a very useful classification. A whorl is accidental if it's made up of any two kinds of pattern—except the plain arch. If a fingerprint doesn't look like any of the patterns, it's called an accidental whorl too.

In a double loop, one loop flows from one side of your finger and the other flows from the other side. The loops curve around each other in the centre.

When you've figured out what kind of fingerprint you have on the tape, look at the fingerprints on your other fingers. Don't forget your thumbs! If you shake some talcum powder onto your fingertip then gently smooth off the extra powder, you'll be able to see the ridges better.

The lines or ridges in fingerprints do all sorts of funny things. They stop, they split into two parts. You might see a short ridge,

or one so small it's just a dot or island.

A lake is made when a ridge splits into two, then joins together again.

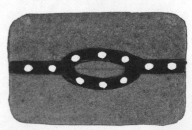

36

A spur is a part of a ridge that curves backwards.

A crossover looks like the route a train takes when it crosses over from one track to another.

You know whom your fingerprints belong to, but who owns the fingerprint found at the scene of the crime? To find out, detectives compare it with all the fingerprints in a fingerprint library. Police departments save fingerprints of people who have been arrested, and share these records with other departments. The largest fingerprint library in North America belongs to the Federal Bureau of Investigation. It contains over 107,000,000 sets of fingerprints!

Today, computers can be programmed to look for

fingerprint matches a lot faster than people can. All those things ridges do—the lakes, the islands, the crossovers—are called minutiae. The minutiae are mapped and measured, then fed into the computer, which looks for a match at the rate of 4000 comparisons a second. Searches that used to take days, weeks or even months are finished in seconds or minutes.

FINGERPRINT KEYS

In the future, you may use your fingerprint to open doors, start your car or even take out money at a bank machine.

Your fingerprint will act as a key. You'll press your finger or thumb on a special pad. The pad will be connected to a computer that scans or reads the fingerprint, then compares the information with data stored in its memory bank. If it gets a match, hey presto, the door opens, the car starts or the money flows.

Security systems based on fingerprints are called biometric. "Bio" has to do with living things. "Metric" has to do with measurements. The computer uses measurements to compare living things, like your fingerprints. A fingerprint makes a great key: you'll never lose it and it can't be stolen or copied.

Hanging on

Your hands go into action the moment you wake up. They grab, push, turn, pull. Think of some of the things they handle before you get out the front door. Bedcovers, light switch, doorknob, taps, soap, toothbrush, buttons, zippers, laces, cereal box, refrigerator door, milk jug, orange juice jar, bowl, spoon. And, if you're also rushing to finish off last night's homework, pens, pencils and erasers.

Your fingers and thumbs work together when you handle things, and you can hang on to things in different ways.

Take a tour around the house and collect a hammer, a pencil, a key, a suitcase (or a briefcase with a handle) and a jar with a screw top.

Now grab them, one at a time.

Hold the key as if you were going to unlock a door. You're holding it in—surprise—a **key grip**. Your fingers are lined up to make a solid wall on one side of the key. Your thumb presses up against the key on the other side to keep it in place. You use the same kind of grip when you hold a mug.

When you pick up the hammer, you wrap your fingers around the handle. Your thumb presses down on the top side. This **power grip** is a strong, steady grip, good for holding tools or hanging on to things tightly.

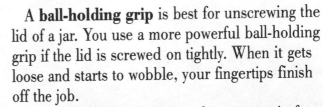

A **hook grip** is a strong grip that can carry a heavy suitcase for a long time. If you can't find a suitcase, go outside and hang by your fingers from the branch of a tree. That's a hook grip too.

Now pick up the pencil. You're holding it between your index and middle fingers and your handy opposable thumb. You use the **precision grip** for fine delicate work, when you want to get some detail just right. Because you can hold things between the big sensitive pad on your thumb and the sensitive pads at the tips of your other fingers, you're good at handling and learning about all kinds of small objects.

A **ball-holding grip** is best for unscrewing the lid of a jar. You use a more powerful ball-holding grip if the lid is screwed on tightly. When it gets loose and starts to wobble, your fingertips finish off the job.

Now see how it feels to use the wrong grip for some familiar objects. Try the power grip on a pencil, or a hook grip to pick up a small object from a table. Your hands are usually so skilful because they can handle different things in different ways.

Grasping hands

Can you imagine what it would be like if you could hang on with your feet as well as your hands? Your opposable thumb helps you grasp with your hands. If you had an opposable big toe, you could grasp with your feet as well. Most apes and monkeys have opposable thumbs—like you do—and opposable toes too! Their hands are good at grasping and hanging on and some of them have hands that are good at picking up and handling things.

Orangutans are sometimes called four-handed because they are so clever with their feet. Since they're the heaviest inhabitants of the trees, they need lots of grip to stay up there.

Spider monkeys swing through the branches of their South American rainforest home. The monkey's thumb and finger grip isn't very good, so it has a strong "fifth hand," a prehensile tail that can wrap around things and hold on.

The great apes—orangutans, chimpanzees and gorillas—have short thumbs, but they are fully opposable. The fingers and palms of their hands are bare and sensitive, so they are good for feeling as well as grasping. A chimpanzee might pick up a stick and poke it into a hole to see who's there—then run off if he disturbs bees! Gorillas peel celery stalks and groom each other to find dry skin or burrs. One gorilla even tore apart a scientist's notebook a page at a time.

Monkeys and apes have to use their hands for climbing and walking, as well as their feet. You are the only primate who walks upright on your feet, so your hands are totally free to do all kinds of things.

Famous hands quiz

1. How many fingers does Mickey Mouse have?

2. Which famous magician is said to have his hands insured for $3 million?

3. Which monsters have hairs on the palms of their hands?

4. Who lost his hand to a crocodile?

5. What is the name of the gorilla who can talk with her hands?

6. What famous escape artist was called the Handcuff King?

7. Which Queen of England had six fingers on one hand?

8. What famous couple danced hand in hand on the edge of the sand?

8. The owl and the pussycat from Edward Lear's poem.

7. Anne Boleyn, the second wife of King Henry VIII of England, had the beginning of a sixth finger with a double nail on one of her hands.

6. Handcuff King was the nickname for Harry Houdini.

5. Her name is Koko, and she speaks sign language.

4. Captain Hook in the story of Peter Pan.

3. Werewolves have hairy palms.

2. Doug Henning, of course.

1. Four. Three fingers and a thumb. Most cartoon characters are missing a finger. It's hard to draw hands that don't look like bunches of bananas.

41

Other Hands

Have you ever watched your cat playing with a marble, batting it around with his front paw? Or a squirrel nibbling a snack he's holding? There are many kinds of hands in the animal world. The hands of apes and monkeys look a lot like yours, but other animal hands are hidden inside wings and flippers. The hands of different animals may have a similar arrangement of bones, but they don't always look alike. Because hands suit the needs of their owners, some hands are good for running and some for swimming. Other hands fly.

Hands that run and walk

Some animals run and walk on their hands and feet. Use your own hand to see how.

Put your hand down flat on the table. Pretend your arm is an animal's limb. When your fingers and the palm of your hand are flat you're imitating the earliest way of walking; it's the flat-footed stance. Some animals, like bears and apes, walk this way. So do you!

Raise your palm up from the table, but keep your fingers flat. Animals who walk and run this way put all their weight on the ends of their metacarpals (the bones of the palm of the hand) and their metatarsals (the long bones of the foot). This way of walking—on the digits—is called digitigrade. It's a springy kind of walk. Rabbits run like this, and so does your cat or dog.

Raise your hand up until only the tips of your fingers and thumb are touching the table. Lift up your little finger and thumb. You're standing the way a rhinoceros does on three fingers or toes, digits two, three and four.

When you lift up digit number two, your index finger, you're standing like a camel, on digits three and four.

And when you lift up your ring finger, digit four, you're standing on your middle finger, digit three. Now you're a horse.

Horses didn't always stand on their middle fingers and toes. Eohippus, who lived about 50 million years ago, had four digits on its front legs and three digits on its back legs. Early horses needed digits that could spread out to stop them sinking into the mud of the swampy ground. As time passed and the swampy ground dried up, horses didn't need to have spread-out digits. Today's horses have only one digit with a tough hoof on the end (like your fingernail), but they still have left-over bits of digit two and digit four in their legs.

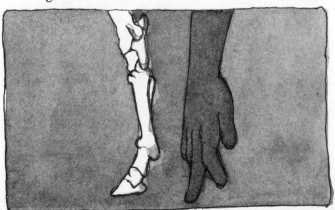

Hands that swim

Plesiosaurs rowed themselves through the water using their broad flippers like oars. Plesiosaurs often had extra phalanges (finger bones) to make their flippers into more efficient paddles.

You can't see a dolphin's finger bones because they're inside its flippers. Dolphins have added phalanges to their fingers too, but only the third and fourth digits have extra bones.

Hands that fly

Flying reptiles called Pterosaurs had three free digits with claws. The fourth digit had four very long finger bones that supported the wing membrane.

Bats fly with their fingers. They've been doing it for 50 million years. The wing membranes are supported by the bat's arms, legs, tail and the four very long fingers of each hand. The thumb is a sharp little hook with a claw halfway down the wing.

43

High-tech hands

You tried to get along without your thumbs when you taped them to the sides of your hands. You saw what happened when you taped over your fingerprints—you didn't have any traction on your fingertips. Can you imagine what it would be like to be without a whole hand?

At one time, people missing a hand were like Captain Hook in Peter Pan. Their steel hooks were working tools but they didn't look anything like real hands.

Today you might walk right past someone with a myoelectric artificial hand without noticing anything unusual. Did you notice the girl's myoelectric hand in the illustration below? A myoelectric hand looks like a real hand on the outside. The metal structure inside is covered with a plastic glove that matches the person's skin. (It doesn't tan in the summer, though.)

Inside the plastic hand are metal fingers. Here's how they move. The myoelectric hand is attached to the lower arm. It has a battery to make the fingers move and an electronic processor. When the person wants to open or close the hand, she contracts the muscles in her lower arm. The contraction produces a signal that closes or opens the hand. A strong muscle contraction opens the hand, and a gentle one closes it. Only the thumb and first two fingers are powered. The other fingers just follow along.

Toddlers as young as 16 months are fitted with myoelectric hands. They're too small to be taught how they work, but toddlers are good at exploring, and in a little while they figure out how to make the hand open and close.

Myoelectric hands are electric, so they must not get wet. But having a myoelectric hand won't get you out of doing the dishes—you just have to make sure the water doesn't go higher than the plastic glove. You might break a dish if you hang on too hard, though!

THE CANADHAND?

What kind of hand does the space shuttle's mechanical Canadarm have? It doesn't have fingers or a thumb—not even mechanical pincers. The "fingers" are three movable wires that criss-cross to make a triangle shape. When the wires move, the triangle shape gets bigger or smaller. The wires of the Canadarm's "hand" close on a post sticking out from a satellite to catch it in space. This kind of hand was designed to take hold and let go without a pushing movement that might send the payload tumbling off into space.

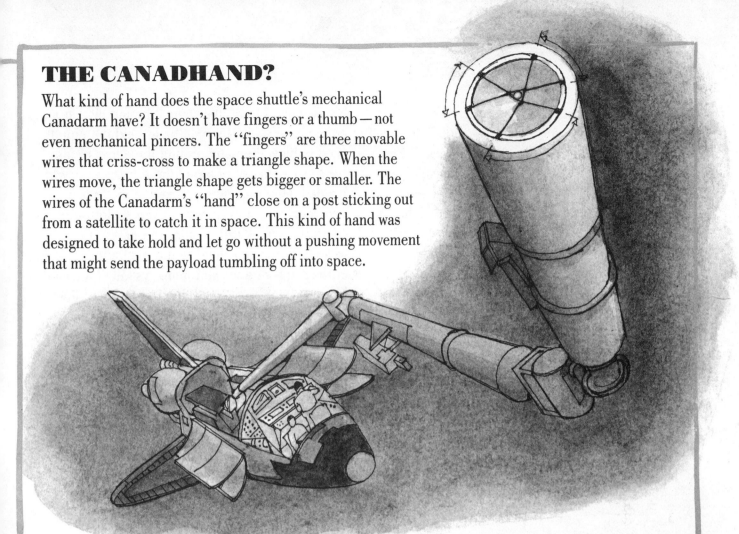

A SILLY SHAKE

A handshake uses a power grip. Just don't make it too powerful. Try this silly shake.

Shake hands in the usual way, but squeeze your friend's hand regularly like a heartbeat. Say, "Hello, I'm from the Heart Foundation."

If you liked this silly shake, there are more on page 71.

Lefties

If you're left-handed, you're part of a small minority. Most of the world is right-handed. There have always been more righties than lefties. Scientists have studied the stencils (outlines) of hands made 30,000 years ago by Cro-Magnon peoples in the caves of Spain and France. Eight out of ten were of the left hand. If the artist used

his own hand to do the stencil, he put his left hand on the cave wall. His right hand held the pipe he used to blow the paint around the edges of his hand, so eight out of ten of the artists were right-handed. Other scientists looked at pictures of people in drawings, paintings and sculpture from 15,000 B.C. to 1950. In nine out of ten, the weapon or tool was held in the right hand. A study of the skulls of apes and monkeys killed for food by early peoples showed that most of the blows were struck by the right hand.

Scientists don't really know why most people are righties. There are lots of theories though.

The tools of early people were nearly always made for the right hand. They were precious possessions that were handed down from one generation to the next. If you inherited a right-handed tool, you had to use it with your right hand, even if you were a natural leftie. Some people believe that this encouraged right-handedness.

Perhaps most people used their right hand to hold a sword because they held their shield in their left hand to protect their heart.

Most people agree that it's easier to be right-handed in a right-handed world. Scissors and can-openers are right-handed. Ladles with spouts pour only when they're held in your right hand. When you go through a subway turnstile, you have to put your money or token in with your right hand. So the environment helps decide which hand a person will use.

and righties

Many lefties have left-handed parents. Maybe they inherited their left-handedness, or maybe they live in a more left-handed world because of their left-handed parents.

If you're a boy, you're more likely to be left-handed. You might be very artistic, athletic or gifted in math. And if you're a twin, you're twice as likely to be left-handed.

So what's it like being a leftie? If you're a leftie, you're part of a minority — and minorities often have a hard time.

Language has always put down lefties. The left is considered the weaker side. The left hand is also considered clumsy, awkward and inept. A "left-handed compliment" is just the opposite of praise, and if you give someone "the left hand of friendship," you're not being friendly at all, unless you're a Boy Scout. The Latin word for left is "sinister." It has come to mean suspicious, dishonest, even evil. The French word for left, "gauche," means clumsy and awkward in English.

On the right side, things are different. The right is the stronger side. It's an honour to be placed on someone's right-hand side. If you're a "right-hand man or woman," you're the best and most trustworthy assistant. The word dextrous comes from the Latin word "dexter," which means right. If you're dextrous, you're skilful and clever.

If you're equally at home using your left hand or your right, you're ambidextrous — both your hands work like right hands. The ambidextrous artist Sir Edwin Landseer once proved that it is possible to draw two things at the same time. He called for two pencils and a sheet of paper. Then, at the same time, he drew the head of a stag with antlers with one hand and the head of a horse with the other.

It is useful to be able to change hands if one gets tired or hurt, but if you're ambidextrous don't get too smug. The word also means double-dealing or two-faced!

47

LEFT-RIGHT

Do you think you're totally right-handed or left-handed? Not many people are, although lefties are often more skilful with their right hands than righties are with their left. Here's part of a left-right test used by Desmond Morris. Try it to see whether you're more right-sided or more left-sided.

When you have an itch in the middle of your back, which hand does the scratching?

When you interlock your fingers, which thumb is on top?

When you put your hands behind your back, which hand holds onto the other?

When you cross your arms, which arm is on top?

When you clap your hands, which hand is on top?

When you count to three on the fingers of one hand, which index finger does the counting?

The next time you stir your hot chocolate, see whether the spoon goes in a clockwise or anti-clockwise direction. Lefties often stir in an anti-clockwise direction. Righties stir the other way.

WRITE TO LEFT

Most people write from left to right, but some people, like the artist and inventor Leonardo da Vinci, often wrote backwards from right to left. Backwards writing is like a secret code—you can only read it if you hold it up to a mirror. That's why it's sometimes called mirror writing.

Try writing your name backwards. Start at the right-hand side of your page. If you're a leftie like Leonardo, it might be easier for you.

Here's another way to mirror write. Hold an index card up against your forehead. Now write your name. Be sure to start on the left side of your forehead. Close your eyes and "see" what you're doing. In your mind's eye, the writing looks right. But when you take the index card off your forehead, you're in for a surprise. Your writing is backwards. Check it out in the mirror to see how you did.

LEFTIES FIGHT BACK

Lefties have to adjust to a right-handed world, but sometimes they have the last laugh. Elias Howe, the inventor of the sewing machine, was left-handed. He put the needle of the sewing machine where it was handy for him—on the left side—and that's where it stayed. So generations of right-handed sewers have learned to sew left-handed.

SOUTHPAWS

Why are left-handed pitchers called southpaws? In many ballparks, home plate is located towards the west or the south, so that the sun doesn't shine in the batter's eyes. When home plate is towards the west, a pitcher facing home plate has one hand on her north side and one hand on her south side. Her left hand is on the south side, so she throws with her south paw.

In touch

If you're having a bad day, you might put salt instead of sugar on your porridge, walk out the door and see an elephant charging towards you, hear the screeching of brakes, smell something burning when you're making lunch, and touch a hot pot at dinner time. But your senses tell you what's going on in the world around you and what to do about it, so you taste that white stuff before you put it on your porridge, run away from the elephant, stop when you hear the car brakes, rescue your grilled cheese sandwich, and jerk your hand away from the hot pot.

People used to think that there were only five senses: sight, hearing, smell, taste and touch. But the skin can sense things in more than one way, so when you reach out to touch something or it touches you, you learn how hard it's pressing against you, if it's hot or cold, and whether it hurts.

The skin senses can be fooled though. They stop sending messages if the input stays the same and send out new messages only when things change. That's why you don't feel the pressure of your clothes on your skin, or the gloves on your hands —unless you move, that is. The movement makes the clothes press on your skin in a different way, so you're aware of them—until you get used to the new way they feel.

How does the skin send messages? Under the surface of your skin are nerve endings that are the beginning of a huge communications network called the nervous system.

Nerve endings don't all look the same. Some are flat and others are onion-shaped. Free nerve endings look like straight branches that stick straight up. All these nerve endings are ready and waiting to react to input from the outside world.

Each nerve ending has its own territory, so different spots on the skin of your hand respond to different kinds of input. Pain has the most spots, followed by pressure, then cold, then warmth.

Scientists used to think that each kind of nerve ending responded to only one kind of input. But now they know that some nerve endings are sensitive to more than one kind of stimulus. For example, a nerve ending may react to both temperature and pressure.

The nerve endings, or "receptors," in the skin are attached to long nerve fibres. They're like long wires that carry messages from the skin all the way to the spinal cord and on to the brain. Other messages travel away from the brain and spinal cord. They travel along different nerve fibres and tell the muscles and glands what to do. Nerve cells in the skin talk to other nerve cells—they receive messages and pass them on. All nerve pathways are one-way roads.

That's Hot!

What kinds of messages travel up and down your nerve fibres when you touch a hot pot?

First, the sensory nerve endings in your skin that respond to warmth react—scientists say they "fire." When they fire, they send out a wave of energy, or an "impulse." The impulse zaps along nerve pathways as fast as 100 m (109 yards) a second. It roars up your arm, around your armpit and arrives at your spinal cord.

As soon as the incoming message reaches the spinal cord, it triggers a response. This time the nerve cells that control your muscles "fire." The outgoing message speeds away from the spinal cord using different nerve pathways. This message tells the muscles in your hand and arm to move, and your hand jerks away.

Your body is built so that you pull away when you touch something hot. It's a reflex action. You don't have to think about it, so the message doesn't have to go all the way to your brain. It's acted on as soon as it gets to the spinal cord.

Meanwhile, what's happening to the brain? Part of the message does continue on to the brain to let it know what's happening. The brain also gets messages back from the muscles. So it hears both sides of the story—the information from the senses that came roaring in and information about the movement that was the body's answer.

If you pick up a very hot pot, pressure receptors might respond, as well as heat receptors—and probably pain receptors, too! When lots of nerve cells get involved and send messages to the brain, the brain knows there's a big problem.

BAG IT!

Try this test to see how the skin on your hands reacts to different kinds of pressure. All you need is a sink full of water and a plastic bag big enough for your hand.

1. Put one hand in the plastic bag.

2. Put the hand without the bag in the water. The water is pressing on your hand but you can't feel it as long as you keep your hand still.

3. Now put the hand with the bag into the water. Wow! All of a sudden you can feel the pressure of the water. The plastic bag seems to be glued to your hand.

What makes the difference? Without the bag, the water pressure is the same all around your hand, so the skin senses don't send out any messages. When the water presses on the bag, the bag presses on your hand, and the pressure receptors notice the pressure in a different way.

WHAT IS IT?

I went to the wood and I got it;
I sat down and I looked for it;
I had to bring it home in my hand,
Because I couldn't find it.
And when I found it,
I threw it away.

A. A splinter.

52

HOT OR COLD?

Trick some nerve endings and fool your skin about what's hot and what's cold.

1. Fill a sink with warm water and put your hand in. How warm does it feel? Leave your hand in the water for ten seconds. Now how warm does the water feel? The sensory receptors that react to heat get used to the temperature and stop sending messages when it doesn't change.

2. Stick your other hand into the basin. Does the water feel warmer?

Try this experiment with a basin of cold water. What happens?

SOMETHING TO THINK ABOUT

You've just played an amazing game of baseball. You stole a base, slid into home, and caught a fly ball. You ended up sprawled on the ground, but the ball was in your glove. Now the game's over and you have time to pay attention to some of the messages that have been trying to get through to your brain.

Your elbow hurts. You check it out and see a scrape. When did that happen? And there's a little ache in your left ankle, as if you twisted it. Why didn't you notice these aches and pains before?

Scientists know that how you're feeling has a lot to do with how much you're aware of pain. You notice pain more if you're listening hard to the pain receptors in your body.

Try wiggling your toes while you're in the dentist's chair and twiddling your thumbs at the same time. If your brain is thinking hard about your toes and your thumbs, it can't pay as much attention to what's going on in your mouth.

Your smart hands

Your friend has come to show you a new puzzle. He's holding it in his hand and fiddling with it. You say, "Can I see it?" Of course, you can see it perfectly well. It's right in front of your eyes. What you mean is, "Can I handle it?"

You can learn a lot about something by holding it in your hands, or running your hands over its surface. Is it heavy? Light? Rough? Smooth? Do the parts move? How does it work?

Your fingertips are the second most sensitive part of your body. The tip of your tongue has 200 pressure points per square centimetre (that's 1300 per square inch). Each of your fingertips has about half that many. Funny thing, though—your fingertips can feel your pulse in your wrist, but your tongue can't!

Those sensitive fingertips—and the rest of your hand—are so smart, they can see around corners and in the dark.

To test out your talented hand, find a nice dark place; a pocket will do. Fill it with things to identify: a quarter, a piece of string, a sticky leftover candy, a key, a small stone. You may already have a pocket loaded up and ready to go. Stick your hand in and rummage around. Grab something. Can you tell what's what just by feeling it and moving it around in your hand? Scientists call this ability to recognize things by handling them the stereognostic sense.

Your hands are not only smart at identifying things; they're also good at learning things. When you want to learn something new such as how to juggle or how to do string games, your brain has to tell your hands what to do every step of the way. But after you've repeated a move lots of times,

something strange happens. Your hands seem to take over, and you juggle or make string figures without thinking about what you're doing. The more you practise, the better you'll get. (Rest periods are important, too. Don't overdo it.)

When you're learning a skill that involves your hands (called a motor skill), repeat it often so that it becomes a habit. You'll remember how to do it for a long time, longer than you remember historical facts or the words of a poem.

Want a new muscle-learning challenge? Find a friend and try the ten-step hand clapping game on page 108.

NINE TIMES

Your fingers are so smart they can help you learn the nine times table. Here's how it works.

Put your hands on the table in front of you. Your fingers are numbered 1 to 10. The left little finger is 1. The right little finger is 10. To multiply 9 × 3, tuck under finger number three. It's the middle finger on your left hand. The tens in your answer are to the left of the finger you've tucked under. The units are to the right. You can see the answer. It's 27.

Now try it with 9 × 5. Tuck under finger number 5, your left thumb, and read the answer on your fingers: 45.

This works from 1 × 9 to 9 × 10. You have to learn 9 × 11 and 9 × 12. Sorry!

HERE'S FINGER NUMBER 3 TUCKED UNDER.

READING WITH YOUR FINGERTIPS: BRAILLE

Your hands are so smart that they can take over for some of your other senses if necessary. A person who can't see reads by moving her sensitive fingertips across the dots in a Braille book. You might say she can "see" with her fingers.

Braille was developed by Louis Braille when he was only 15 years old. When he was a student at a school for the blind in Paris, he heard about a way of writing letters using raised dots. Charles Barbier, who had invented the dot system, used to send and receive dot messages on the battlefield. Because you didn't need a light to write or read the dots, you didn't attract the enemy's attention. Barbier called his system nocturnal (night) writing.

But Barbier's 12-dot system was too complicated to remember, and too big to read with fingertips. So Louis Braille improved the system. He never used more than six dots for each letter space or "cell." And he used letters, not sounds, so that words could be spelled correctly.

Every single letter in a Braille book must be translated into dots. All these dots take a long time to read, and Braille books are very bulky. Short forms and contractions speed up the reading process and make the books shorter.

The word "wing," for example, has four letters, but in Braille it has only two characters: the dot pattern for "w" and the dot pattern for "ing." The dot pattern for "g" is also the word "go." "You" is the letter "y."

There are signs for commas, periods and other punctuation marks. And there's a number sign. Altogether, there are 63 different dot patterns.

You read Braille by moving your fingertips from left to right, the way you read print, across the lines of dots. But when you write Braille by hand, you write the other way, from right to left, just like mirror writing. When you try writing your name in Braille, you'll see why.

Here are the Braille dot patterns for the letters a to z and the one for capital letters.

56

WRITE YOUR NAME IN BRAILLE

You'll need some graph paper and a sharp pencil or a ballpoint pen.

1. Make boxes for your dots. Each box should be three squares high and two squares across. In Braille, these boxes are called cells. Each cell has room for six dots.

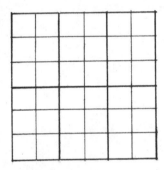

2. Write your name in Braille dots from left to right. Braille is a code, so look up the letters you need on the chart. Don't forget to put the character for capital letter in the first cell.

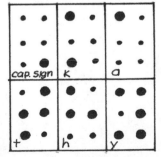

3. Turn the graph paper over. You should be able to see the dots through the paper. Start from the right side this time and go over the dots with your pen or pencil. Press firmly so that the dots stand out on the other side. This is the way Braille is written by hand. Turn the paper over again to feel the Braille characters with your fingertips.

Braille can also be typed on a Brailler. This mechanical device works like a typewriter, but it has only six keys, one for each dot. To make a character, you press down the keys for the dots you need, all at the same time.

The next time you're at the public library, ask if they have Braille books in their collections. Some Braille books have the text in Braille and in writing that you can read as well. You might find one of your favourite stories. If you do, you can try breaking the code. See if you can figure out some of the words.

The last word on handworks

Pinkety, pinkety

Here's a way to make a wish come true—at least this is how they used to do it in Glasgow, Scotland, according to Iona and Peter Opie.

You and a friend link pinkies, then press your thumbs together.

Chant:
Pinkety. pinkety, thumb to thumb,
Wish a wish and it's sure to come.
If yours comes true
Mine will come true,
Pinkety, pinkety, thumb to thumb.

There's My Thumb

In Scotland, two people sealed a bet or a bargain this way. They licked their thumbs, then pressed the wet thumb balls together. This made the bet or bargain binding and was taken very seriously.

In 1642 a Scottish lieutenant licked his thumb to pledge himself to a duel—in which he was killed. More than 300 years later, children in England were still licking their thumbs to seal bets or dares.

SOAPY FRIENDSHIPS

Here's a superstition from Alabama that will guarantee long-lasting friendships. Wash your hands with your friends. While you're scrubbing off the dirt say, "Wash together, friends forever." But don't dry your hands together on the same towel because, "Dry together, fuss forever."

HANDTALK

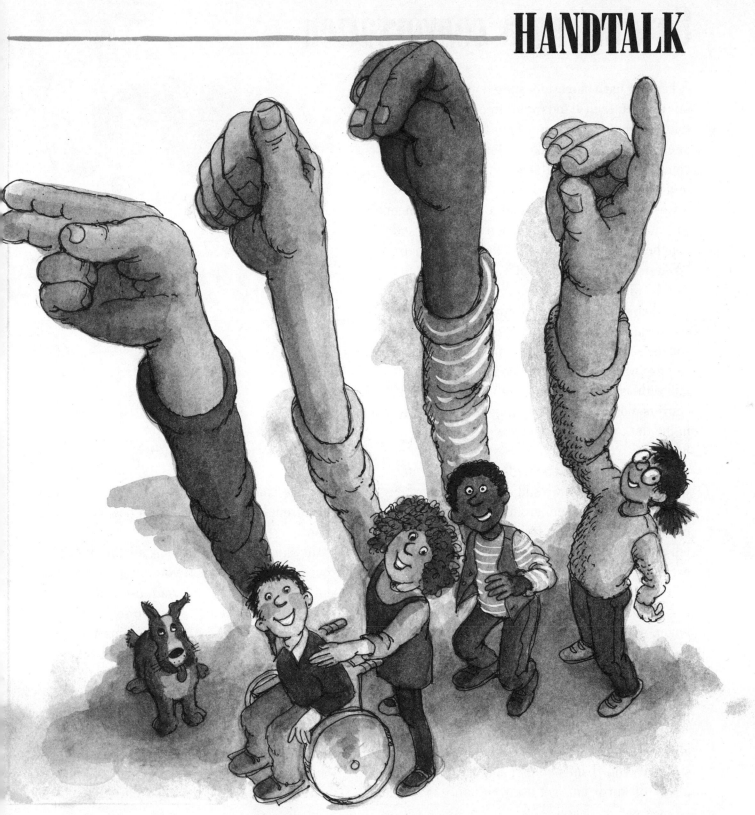

Conducting a conversation

When our early ancestors started to walk upright on two feet, their hands were free to do other things. People could carry food from one place to another. They could make and use tools. And they could communicate with each other using actions or gestures.

Gestures—actions that send a signal to someone watching—were important when people worked together. "Bring that here," "Put it down there," "You dropped it on my foot" might have been "said" with hand gestures.

Perhaps one day hand gestures weren't enough, so over a long period of time, people started to use sounds—to speak. Or maybe people's hands were so busy with tools that they couldn't use them to talk with as well. And you can't have a gesture conversation when there's a big tree in the way, or in the dark when you can't see your friend's hands!

Today we use spoken words to communicate with each other, but we still use our hands when we talk. We wave them around in the air a lot, especially when we are trying to win an argument, tell a funny joke or describe something really exciting.

We use hand gestures to conduct a conversation just the way an orchestra conductor uses his baton, so anthropologists call them "baton gestures." These gestures are unconscious; we don't think about them, but we use them to make a point, stop an interruption, or tell how we're feeling.

Some people gesture wildly with their hands, and some don't. You may be good with words and still wave your hands about a lot, or you may be at a loss for words and not use your hands to fill the

gap. The kind of person you are and where you come from have a lot to do with how you use your hands.

The situation you are in has a lot to do with how your hands move, too. If you are in a noisy room and it's difficult to hear, you'll use your hands a lot more. Or if you are talking to someone who speaks a different language, you'll probably use more hand gestures than usual to make sure you're understood. And if you are having an argument, or trying to persuade someone that you are right and he or she is wrong, you'll put some of the force of your feelings into your hands. In fact, we are so used to using our hands that we wave them about when we're on the phone, even though the person on the other end of the line

can't see the visual messages we're sending.

Next time you talk to someone, watch her hands. Hand positions can tell you a lot about how your friend is feeling. Are her hands closed in powerful fists that beat the air? The Power Grip is a strong grip that uses your whole hand. It's for holding a hammer or hanging on when you're climbing. So if your friend's hands are clenched tightly into fists, she feels pretty strongly about what she's saying. Are the tips of her fingers and thumb gently touching? Perhaps only the tips of her index finger and thumb touch. The Precision Grip is used for holding small things, such as a pencil or a needle. This kind of work is detailed and delicate. If her hands are held in the air in a Precision Grip, she's trying to let you know *exactly* how she feels. Or

maybe she's asking you to make your point clearer and more precise.

Hands can stop you from butting in by pushing you away palms out.

Hands extended out towards you palms down can say, "Hey, wait a minute, calm down."

Hands towards you palms up ask you to agree. "Don't you feel the same way?"

So our hands poke, beat, chop and dance in the air telling the world how we feel when we talk.

THE DOG ATE MY HOMEWORK

Just for fun, think about how your hands might move if you were explaining to your teacher how your dog grabbed your homework and ran away with it.

Tell her how you chased him up and down the street,

while he dashed ahead of you, under hedges, between parked cars (of course, you stopped and didn't run out between the cars), over low fences (you jumped, too).

Tell her that in the end, he ate it and there was nothing you could do except shake your finger at him.

Your hands will probably show her his route—up, over, through. They'll tell her how you felt as you chased him—and how you felt as you watched him eat it with relish—that's with pleasure, not the green stuff you put on hotdogs.

Put lots of energy into your story, and you might get off lightly this time!

CROSS YOUR FINGERS

When you cross your fingers, you are making a very ancient gesture. The crossed fingers were a symbol for the Christian cross. Long ago, Christians thought they could protect themselves from evil by making a cross with their fingers. Because this cross was small, people could make it secretly. We still make it secretly when we cross our fingers behind our backs if we are not telling the truth.

We usually cross our fingers to ask for good luck or when we're hoping that good luck will continue for us or for others. Here are some other reasons for keeping your fingers crossed.

- Some people say that a wish gets trapped where the fingers meet at the centre of a cross. The wish can't escape until it comes true.

- It's supposed to be unlucky to pass someone on the stairs. You may escape the bad luck if both of you cross your fingers!

- If you cross your fingers when you walk under a ladder, the painter might not knock a pot of paint onto your head!

POINTER POWER

We're all taught that it's not polite to point, but we baton a lot with our index fingers. Desmond Morris, an anthropologist who watches people, says that when we shake a raised forefinger at someone, we're really hitting him over the head with an imaginary stick.

If someone stops you to ask where the bus stop is, you probably point to it with your forefinger. It's strange but true— the farther away the object, the higher you'll point. It's almost as if you're shooting an arrow from the end of your finger, and you have to aim it higher so that it will go farther.

Never point to a ship at sea, it's bad luck—for the ship, not you!

This pointing finger says, "Here's something important." The hand usually has a decorative cuff at the wrist, like the lace cuff on a bishop's robes, so it's called a Bishop's Cuff or Fist.

Instead of words: emblems

Baton gestures are illustrators—they go along with words. But some hand gestures replace words. These hand gestures are called "emblems." Every place and culture has its own emblems. A gesture that you know and use may have a totally different meaning somewhere else.

What happens when two people have different gesture vocabularies?

Here's an example: You meet a friend. He can talk to you, but you have laryngitis. You have to "talk" with your hands. Here's what he says and what you gesture.

HE SAYS:

"How are you?"

YOU GESTURE:

"Okay."

You make the Okay symbol, but you don't realize that this gesture can also mean "zero."

"Zero? You feel nothing?"

"Everything is just fine."

You make the Thumbs-Up signal. Some people think that Thumbs Up comes from the old Roman gesture made by the people after a gladiator fight. They say that Thumbs Down meant that the audience did not want the losing gladiator to be spared. Thumbs Up meant, "Spare him, he fought a good fight."

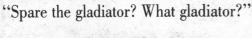

"Spare the gladiator? What gladiator?"

"I can't believe what I'm hearing."

You tug your ear. This conversation is getting out of hand. The Ear Tug can be used as a warning: there's someone listening to our conversation. It can be a sign of praise, or a sign of disbelief. That's the way you've used it, but your friend doesn't understand.

"What's the matter with your ear?"

"You're crazy!"

You use your index finger to make circles in the air beside your head. Another way of saying "You're crazy!" with gestures is to tap your temple (that's your forehead right beside your eye) with your index finger to say "There's something wrong inside." The crazy gesture you used, though, has another meaning in the Netherlands. And that's the one your friend knows. He asks:

"A phone call for me? I didn't hear the phone ring."

You both shake your heads and walk off in opposite directions.

You've probably never had a conversation quite like this, but it's easy to see how different gesture vocabularies can create misunderstandings.

65

YES, BUT THAT'S RUDE

Did you ever put your thumb on your nose and waggle your fingers at someone? Maybe you even added on your other hand by joining the thumb of your second hand onto the little finger of your first hand. Your action says, "You can't get me" or "I don't care about you."

The Nose Thumb is one of the best known hand signals, and nearly everybody knows that it's used to tease or mock someone. Some anthropologists think that a medieval jester or fool, Till Eulenspiegel, who travelled in Germany made this gesture popular. They say that he used to mock and jeer at his audience using the nose thumb as an insult.

Most people call this gesture Thumbing the Nose, but it's sometimes called The Five-Finger Salute because it looks like a salute that has slipped. This rhyme was chanted by children in England during the Second World War (be sure to do it with gestures):

Salute the captain of the ship. (Salute)

Sorry, sir, my finger slipped!
(The Nose Thumb)

PALM UP OR PALM DOWN?

If you're in Zimbabwe, Africa, and someone asks you how tall a person is, you show them "This high" with the palm of your hand facing up. It's more respectful than a palm down gesture, which is used only for animals.

Cup your hand and draw a half-circle in the air as shown in the picture. What is it?
Make the bottom half of the circle.
"The other side of this."

Gesture jokes

Put the tips of your fingers and thumbs together, thumb to thumb, index to index and so on. One hand is on top, one hand is underneath. Push your hands away from each other, then spread your fingers and let the palms come close to each other. Do this several times. What is it?
"A spider doing push-ups on a mirror."

Make the Okay sign, tips of index finger and thumb touching, the other fingers extended. Fly your hand by, but make it jump a little now and then. What is it?
"A butterfly with hiccups."

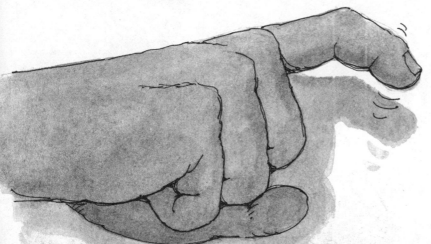

Make a fist. Point your index finger out. Fly your hand through the air, waggling your index finger. What is it?

"I don't know but (fly your hand by, waggling all your fingers and thumb) here comes a whole flock of them."

Waving

You're walking along the street. You hear a car horn honk. You look up and see your friend. His hand is up, palm facing outwards, and he's moving it from side to side. He can't say hello, so he's greeting you from a distance. He's waving, and of course you wave back.

Waving is an open-handed gesture. We show that our open hands are empty — they're not holding any weapons — so we come as friends.

Anthropologist Desmond Morris says that an up and down wave is like a pat on the shoulder, but from a distance. A wave that goes from side to side doesn't pat, but it's much easier to see.

Do you know the story of the people marooned on a desert island? After days and days, they see a cruise ship with people on deck. They jump up

and down and wave their arms in the air. The people on deck smile and wave back in a friendly way, and the ship steams off into the sunset.

The castaways didn't know that a distress wave is different from a greeting. If you're ever stuck on a desert island, raise and lower your outstretched arms, keeping them stiff and straight. The cruise ship will stop and rescue you.

Most people wave with their palms showing, but in Italy a wave often has the palm hidden. It looks like the gesture we make when we beckon

someone nearer. Some people say that the waver is looking forward to seeing you again—that's why the hand seems to be calling you back instead of pushing you away. So if you're in Italy, you may have to decide whether to wave goodbye, or go back!

How you feel has a lot to do with the way you wave, too. If you're half an hour late meeting a friend, your wave will probably not be quite as enthusiastic. And if her wave is a cold little salute, watch out!

HELLO OUT THERE!

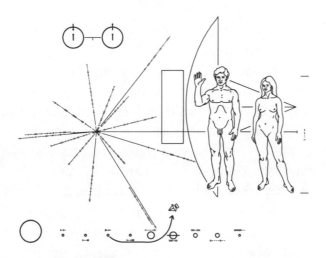

The space probe Pioneer 10, launched March 3, 1972, will be the first man-made object to leave our solar system and enter interstellar space. This gold-plated plaque is attached to the probe. It's a golden greeting card that carries a message from us to any extraterrestrials who find it.

Notice that the woman isn't waving. Scientists didn't want the finders of the plaque to think that all human beings have one arm that is always bent at the elbow!

Scientists hope that this friendly, open-handed gesture will be understood all over the universe. But even if the greeting isn't understood, the gesture does show off our opposable thumbs.

Do you recognize this outer-space wave? This open-handed greeting was used by Mr. Spock on the TV series "Star Trek." Leonard Nimoy, the actor who played Mr. Spock, felt that a special signal was needed when Spock greeted T'Pau, the Matriarch of the planet Vulcan. Not everybody can make their fingers separate this way, but Nimoy could, and so could Celia Lovsky who played T'Pau. The Vulcan greeting was born!

Shaking hands

Today you might wave to a friend or use your own special handshake to say "Hi" or "Bye." Shaking hands is another open-handed gesture of greeting. Of course, some people believe that when you grab an empty right hand to shake it, you're making absolutely sure that hand can't reach for anything dangerous!

You can tell a lot about a person by the way she shakes hands. Everyone has met the Knuckle Cruncher. She grabs your hand, scrunches your fingers in a vice-like grip and pumps your arm up and down. You probably back off a bit—once you can free your hand that is. Watch out, especially if you're wearing rings! Then there's the Dead Fish. A person gives you his hand, then just lets it lie in yours limply.

If you're giving someone the full handshake routine, you probably look her in the eyes and smile or say something about being pleased to meet her. You're saying hello and also letting the person know that you're willing to talk more. If two people fumble around and can't manage to shake hands very well, they probably won't have a very successful conversation either.

A handshake between long-lost friends is very different from a handshake between strangers. According to books of polite manners, a regular handshake is firm and brief. A slightly warmer handshake might last longer, and one person might bring her left hand up to clasp her friend's right hand. A sort-of sandwich handshake. If someone does this to you—and you like her—you might respond by clasping the hand sandwich with your left hand—a sandwich double-decker. Or you might use your left hand to give a friendly squeeze to your friend's arm or shoulder. If you add a

Q. WHAT DO BANANAS DO WHEN THEY MEET EACH OTHER?

A. A BANANASHAKE!

PUP   PET

70

shoulder-squeeze, you're on your way to a hug. Move that hand up to circle round your friend's shoulder, and the shaking hands become the sandwich. Of course, two good friends who haven't met for a long time will probably by-pass all levels of handshakes and just greet each other with open arms, ready for a hug. That's probably the most open-handed gesture of all.

Some groups of people, like the Boy Scouts, have their own special handshake. When Baden-Powell, the founder of the Boy Scouts, was in Africa, he heard the legend of two neighbouring tribes who were always at war. The chief of one of the tribes wanted to stop the fighting, so the next time they met he threw down his weapons and went towards the enemy. He held out his left hand as a sign of friendship and trust. Today Boy Scouts all over the world shake hands with their left hand —the one closer to the heart—as a symbol of trust and brotherhood.

SILLY SHAKES

- Hello, I'm from the Dairy Board. With one hand, hold your friend's index finger. With the other hand, take hold of her little finger. Now pull gently, first with one hand, then with the other, as if you were milking a cow.

- Hello, I'm from the glue factory. Shake hands as usual. Look at a pretend watch and say, "Well, I have to go now." Start to walk away, but don't let go, as if your hand and your friend's are glued together.

- Hello, I'm from NASA. Shake hands but lift yours higher and higher, like a rocket taking off.

- Hello, I'm from the video arcade. Pretend your friend's thumb is a joystick. Use your thumb to push the imaginary button on the top. Now move the thumb around as if you were playing a video game.

- How do lumbermen shake hands? Get a friend and find out. Make a fist, but stick your thumb up, like the Thumbs-Up signal. Your friend grabs your thumb with his hand, but leaves his thumb sticking up. Keep going to add your other hands, then "saw" your joined hands backwards and forwards.

SECRET HANDSHAKES

Do you and your friends have a secret handshake? Maybe your hands dance around each other and clasp in several different ways.

Many kinds of handshakes came out of Black culture in the United States. They were called "soul" shakes. People who shook hands in a certain way were saying more than "Hi." They were telling each other that they felt the same way about a lot of things.

Because these shakes looked cool, lots of people copied them and that's why you and your friends give each other five (that's five fingers, not five dollars!) when something terrific happens, or when someone makes a good point.

Take a friend by the hand and make up your own special handshake. Start off by shaking hands, then grab each other's thumbs. Follow this up by locking your fingers together, or giving each other a High Five. And then finish up by touching knuckles or fists. When you and your friends greet each other like this, you're telling the world you're part of a group.

THE FAR SIDE   By GARY LARSON

© Chronicle Features, 1980

Hey, Zoran! What's happenin'! . . . Give me six!

GIMME SOME SKIN . . .

The skin we're talking about is the skin on the palm of your hand, which touches when two people shake or slap hands. Dictionaries say that "Gimme some skin" was jive talk used by Black musicians in the 1940s in the United States.

In the sixties and seventies, Slap handshakes and High Fives became part of the world of sports, a way for athletes to congratulate each other, or wish each other well. Team members didn't have to stop to give a Slap handshake; they could greet each other on the run.

When you watch sports, see how many different kinds of shakes and congratulations you can spot.

WHY FROG HAS FLAT HANDS

This tale is based on a proverb and story collected in 1930 by anthropologists George Herzog and Charles Blooah from members of the Jabo tribe in Eastern Liberia.

Europeans probably introduced people in West Africa to the custom of shaking hands. Where this story came from, a handshake went like this. Two people shook hands, but as soon as their palms touched they slid their hands apart and snapped their fingers.

Now here's the story. It's about a frog who was more of a person than a frog when this happened.

The person who is Frog had a large farm. But the person who is Frog was so small, that he called on the people of the town to help him clear his field. Many workers came to help Frog. They cleared and cleared the field until they cleared it all. Now Frog wanted to thank each person for his help so he ran ahead of the long line of workers that stretched for miles along the road to town.

When he reached the front of the line, he turned around and stuck out his hand. As the first worker came near, Frog grabbed his hand and shook it enthusiastically, shouting, "Oh, thank you, thank you!" Then he let go and grabbed the hand of the next worker. Again he shouted, "Thank you, thank you!" Frog shook hands and shook hands, and the long line of people shook hands and shook hands with Frog. Now some people in the crowd had very powerful hands, and their handshakes squeezed and squeezed Frog's hands until they were all flattened out.

Frog's hands hurt from all that squeezing, so he went to God to complain. But God said, "Next time you want to thank a large crowd, tell a messenger to announce your thanks all over town at the cock's first crow. And don't you shake hands again with everybody."

This is the reason why Frog's hands are flat, and this is why people sometimes say: Frog says, "Don't shake hands with a crowd."

73

Handclaps

Have you ever given a speech in front of a big crowd? When you finish, there's a moment of silence, then you hear it—the sound of lots of hands hitting against each other. Your audience is clapping to let you know how much they liked you.

Clapping is a gesture that we learn. We all clap at about the same speed so a very slow clap sends a different message: we didn't like this at all. In some countries, though, a slow clap is complimentary.

If you clap a tiny clap, using only your thumbs and clapping your thumbnails together, you're also

changing the gesture to show how little you liked the show.

Handclaps didn't always mean what they mean today. A handclap was used to call a slave or a servant, or to drive a person away—a crowd might "clap" someone out of town.

A legend of the Dene people of Canada's Northwest Territories says that if you clap, whistle and make other loud noises, you'll annoy the spirits of the Northern Lights. The dancing spirits will come closer and closer to scare you!

NOISY HANDS

Why do clapping hands make a loud noise? When you clap, you squeeze air between your moving hands. As your hands come together, the strong squeeze squashes the air into a smaller space. The more the air is squashed together, the harder it pushes on the air next to it. The push travels through the air to your ear, where it presses on your eardrum. The bigger the push, the more pressure on your eardrum, and the louder the sound.

Try bringing your hands together very slowly. Is there any sound? If the air isn't squashed together there's no push to travel to your eardrum.

The next time you're in your bath, try clapping with your hands in the water. The "squirt" of water you make when you bring your hands together is just like the "squirt" of air you make when you clap in the air.

WHOOPS!

Have you ever heard the story of the amazing performing flea? Sometimes she's called Esmerelda, sometimes Philomena. You can call your flea whatever you like. Here's the story and how you tell it.

Hold out your hand towards your audience, palm up. Tell them that Philomena, the amazing flea, will perform for them. Pretend to talk to your flea.

"Dance, Philomena, dance." (Philomena, the invisible, dances!)

"Isn't she wonderful? Do cartwheels, Philomena." (Philomena, the invisible, does cartwheels.)

"Will you sing us a song, Philomena?" (Philomena, who can't be heard, sings.)

"Isn't she wonderful, ladies and gentlemen? Let's give her a big hand."

Clap your hands together enthusiastically. Then realize what you've done.

"Philomena? Are you there, Philomena?"

75

Sign language

Sign language

A group of the !Kung people from the Kalahari Desert in Africa is hunting. One of them sees a bat-eared fox. A call or cry would warn the fox that humans are near, so the hunter silently makes the hand-signal for fox and the other hunters pass on the message.

A hand and arm can shape the head and long neck of an ostrich.

What do these hunters of the Kalahari have in common with construction workers, scuba divers and baseball players? All these people use hand signals to communicate, even though they can talk. Because of the situation, they have to "talk" without words.

76

Under the water

Scuba divers always swim with a buddy. Because a diver can't talk under the water, buddies communicate using hand signals.

Some signals are directional. "Stop," "Going up or down." "Okay," is "I'm okay," and "Are you okay?" It's also used to show that a signal is understood.

Signals such as "I'm out of air" and "I need to buddy breathe" (share air) are especially important. So are hand signs that signal distress.

On the job

A truck has just pulled up to a construction site in Chicago with a load of sand. The driver waits for instructions. It's too noisy to shout to him, and construction workers don't waste time and energy running back and forth with directions. They use hand signals to tell the driver to back up, change direction and stop.

Crane operators and their signalmen use hand signals too. Cranes move all kinds of heavy materials and even other machines. Hand signals make sure that each load is carried safely to the right spot. Everyone on a construction site knows the signals, but sometimes people who work together for a while develop a "shorthand" way of communicating.

Hand signals can also be used to ask the time and tell it. They can even let everyone know when the coffee truck arrives!

At the ballpark

When you watch a baseball game, you see lots of hand signals. One set of signals is obvious and exaggerated—the umpires are letting thousands of noisy enthusiastic fans know what's happening in the game. They signal strikes and balls. They let the crowd know whether a runner is safe or out and if a ball is fair or foul.

But if you watch carefully, you might see some other hand signs. Secret handtalk lets the coach tell the batter to hit, bunt or "take" (not swing at) the next pitch. The catcher signals to the pitcher what pitch to use. The third base coach tells the runner at first to steal. The shortstop lets the outfielders know what pitch is coming.

How do baseball signals work? Each message has its own sign, and the players must know what each sign means. The trick is to disguise the signal with all sorts of other moves and twitchings so that the opposing team can't decode the handtalk.

Here's how a baseball signal might work. The third base coach wants to tell the batter to bunt. First, he touches his left leg with his left hand. Then he

adjusts his cap. He touches his belt buckle, then he touches the letters on his chest with both hands. He touches his face and his right hand goes to his opposite sleeve.

Where's the signal? When he touched his leg and his cap, he sent signals that didn't mean anything. They camouflaged the real signal. Then he touched his belt buckle to give the "key" signal. The key says, "The next signal is the real one." He signalled "bunt" when he touched the letters on his chest with both hands. The next signal was more camouflage and the last signal was a release signal. It told the batter that he could look away.

Baseball signals work best when the coach is a good actor. He must be casual about sending the signs, especially the important one. The batter has to play along too; he watches the coach even after he's received the message to avoid tipping off the other team. Opposing players or coaches could decode the message by looking at the signals and then seeing what the player does right after he looks away.

There are lots of funny stories in baseball folklore about rookie batters who can't seem to understand their signals. The player keeps backing out of the batter's box and looking at his coach. Finally the pitcher yells, "He wants you to bunt, B-U-N-T!"

77

American sign language

Construction workers, scuba divers and baseball players sometimes choose to talk without words, but there are people who can never communicate easily using spoken language. They are deaf or hearing impaired. Because they can't hear words, they use a language of hand signs to talk to each other. In the United States and Canada, this language is called ASL—American Sign Language. (Puerto Ricans use ASL, but they may mouth the words in Spanish.) ASL is the fourth most common

language in the United States, after English, Spanish and Italian. It's "spoken" by more than 500,000 people. There are many other sign languages in the world—BSL (British Sign Language), FSL (French Sign Language), Chinese Sign Language and Danish Sign Language. Today deaf people sign, speak and lip-read.

What does a sign-language conversation look like? For one thing, people don't communicate while they're walking along; they stand still. That's because when you "listen" to someone who is signing, you pay close attention to her face, hands and body language. Look away to see where you're going and you'll miss part of the message. If you don't look away, you risk bumping into things!

The signer may use more than her hands to talk to you. She might say a word as she signs it. Sometimes people make other sounds when they use ASL. They suck in air or make noises with their lips. These sounds are like adjectives and adverbs. They add to the meaning, the way changes in your voice add expression to what you're saying.

All signs are made in the signing space. The signing space is an imaginary circle that's drawn around your head and upper body. It's a little like a blank piece of paper before you write on it.

To make your own signing space, bend your arms a little at the elbows, and put your hands together up above your head.

Draw a half circle with each arm. Your hands will come together in the middle, at your waist.

Now you're ready to say something in ASL. Don't just think of the word. Think about the meaning of the word.

Let's say you wanted to sign the word "right." This word has several meanings and each meaning has a different sign.

RIGHT can mean a direction. "Turn right every time you see an elephant." The sign is . . .

RIGHT can also mean, "I agree with you. You and I feel the same way." Here's the sign . . .

It can also mean, "You're right" or "It's the right answer." Sign it this way . . .

79

You can use the same sign to say, "Right on!" if you really agree that it's right. Just make the sign stronger by bringing your hands together, and popping them off each other.

You might say, "Oh, right," when you finally understand. Here's the sign that shows the light bulb going on in your mind . . .

You can change this sign to say something different. If you flick up your little finger instead of your index finger you're saying, **I understand a little**. If you start with your index finger up and pull it down, you're saying, **I un-understand**. (I understood more before you tried to explain it to me.)

Some signs are easy to figure out because they look like pictures. They're called transparent signs. You can look through them like windows and see what they mean. Many signs depicting animals are transparent. People looked at the

different animals and used their hands to describe what they saw. You can see the elephant's long trunk,

the butterfly's wings,

the spider's many legs

and the cat's whiskers in the handshapes and movements of the ASL signs.

As signs are used, they often become less transparent. They change over time just the way words in a spoken language change. These signs become opaque, like a brick wall. You can't see through them to the meaning. The word "home" is a good example. Home is the place where you eat and sleep. The ASL sign for **home** used to show both these actions. First you made the sign for **eat**, then the sign for **sleep**.

Eat and **sleep** are transparent signs. Then people stopped changing the handshape, and even moved the two signs closer together. Some people still make the **eat** sign in front of their mouths, but others have moved it onto their cheeks. So the modern sign for **home** has become opaque. That is, you can't guess at the meaning.

TIPS FOR SIGNERS

Keep your signing space free from distractions. Flowery Hawaiian shirts and dangly earrings make it harder to see the signs.

Don't sign with a deadpan face. How you look has to match what you're saying. When you sign **angry**, do it with an angry face. If you smile, you'll send a mixed message.

If you're a leftie, you sign with your left hand; righties sign with their right.

Building blocks: how signs work

Every sign has three parts: a **handshape**—the shape of your hand as you make the sign; a **location**—where you make the sign in the signing space; and **movement**—how signs move in the signing space. If you change just one of these, you change the sign. Here's an example. This is the sign for **I love you**. What happens when you change the location and the movement?

When that handshape takes off in the signing space like an airplane leaving the ground, it becomes **fly**.

When the handshape flies along higher up in the signing space, the sign becomes **airplane**.

And when you get to the end of your journey and that same handshape flies down to land on your other outstretched palm, you're signing **airport**.

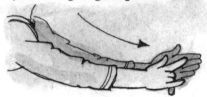

When you change a handshape, but keep the place and the movement, you get a different sign. The sign for **apple** uses the X handshape . . .

and **fruit** uses the F handshape, but the movement and place are the same.

You've already learned the sign for **home**. Keep the same handshape and the same movement, but change the place. Move your hand from one side of your nose to the other to sign **flower**.

Some ideas use two signs. Try signing **son (male + baby)**

and **daughter (female + baby)**.

In some places, **strawberry** is signed **red + secret**. If you've ever looked for tiny wild strawberries, you'll know why!

People who speak ASL have fun with their language too. Here's a sign language joke. This is the sign for **milk**. To make the sign for **pasteurized milk**, use only one hand and move it *past your eyes*. You're allowed to groan.

SQUEEZE

If you're going to stay somewhere **over the weekend**, you walk your fingers from one side of your head, over the top, to the other side—you walk them over your **weak end**—that's your brain!

There's a funny way to say ketchup or catsup. Just make the sign for **cat**, then point up.

SIGN A POEM

Some people have a special talent for interpreting poetry or song in sign language. They communicate what's in the poem or song using their hands, their faces and their body language.

You may have wished upon the first star in the night sky by saying:

Star light, star bright,
First star I see tonight.
I wish I may, I wish I might,
Have the wish I wish tonight.

Here's Irene Kessel's interpretation of the poem in ASL. Notice how ASL doesn't use all the words in each English sentence. Even though it takes twice as long to make and read signs as it does to speak words, a speaker and a signer finish at the same time because ASL says things in a more compact way.

STAR

Make the star sign up to the right in the signing space and look up at it.

BRIGHT

Move your fingers to show the star twinkling.

STAR

FIRST

Point to the star and sign **first** by twisting your wrist inwards. Finish the sign with a little definite move away from you.

STAR

SEE

The sign for **see** moves away from your face up towards the star. Look up at the star.

TONIGHT

Make the horizon with one arm, the flat hand facing down. The other hand shows the sun setting below the horizon.

84

WISH

Make the sign for **wish** and let your breath out at the same time. You want this wish badly.

CAN

This is a strong sign. You still want this wish.

TRULY

What you're saying is really true.

WISH

HAVE

You don't need to say I. Your hands point to yourself.

TONIGHT

BABY SIGN

Deaf babies learn to sign at about the same age that hearing babies start to talk. They might babble sign, the way hearing babies babble at six months. The first sign comes at about a year, at the same time as the first spoken word in hearing children. A deaf baby has to learn how to move his fingers just as the hearing baby has to figure out how to use her voice. Babies begin by making signs that are easier than the ASL signs.

COOKIE

85

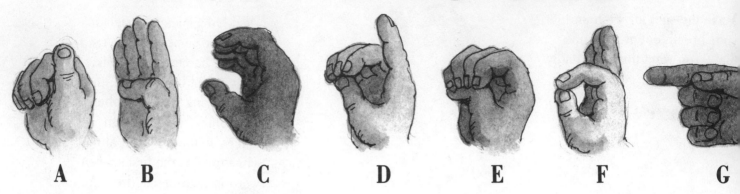

A   B   C   D   E   F   G

People who speak ASL use fingerspelling to spell names and addresses. Technical and scientific words or words that have no sign are fingerspelled too.

Try spelling your name. Each letter of the alphabet has a different handshape. Can you see how some of the handshapes look like the letters when you print them?

Now fingerspell Chicago. You say the word just as you finish fingerspelling it. People who live in Chicago have their own sign for the name of their city. Make the handshape for C (look it up in the alphabet chart). Now move the C-hand across your chest to your right shoulder, then straight down, like two sides of a rectangle.

Do you feel as though you have two left hands (or two right hands if you're a leftie)? It takes lots of practice to talk this way! Fingerspelling is much slower than signing or speaking—it takes three or four times longer to fingerspell a word—so people fingerspell only when they have to.

Helen Keller

Can you imagine having to fingerspell every word you wanted to say letter by letter? Or having to feel with your hands one letter at a time what someone is fingerspelling to you? That's what it was like for Helen Keller. When Helen was small, she had scarlet fever, which left her deaf and blind. She wrote later that she felt as though she were a prisoner in a dark silent world.

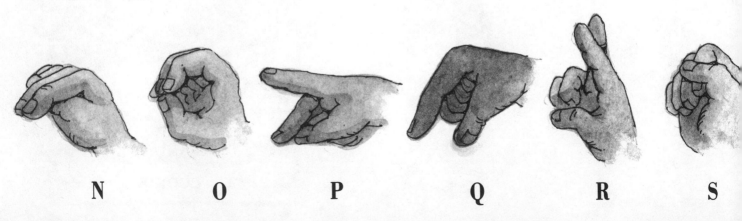

N   O   P   Q   R   S

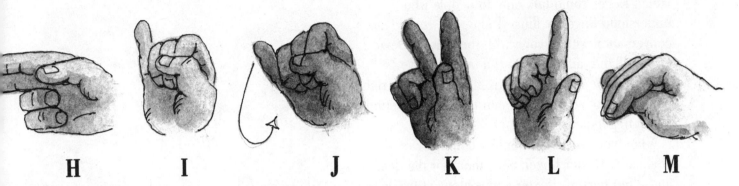

H   I   J   K   L   M

Helen's special teacher, Anne Sullivan, taught Helen by fingerspelling everything into Helen's hand. But Helen didn't understand what Anne was doing until, one day, she realized what the handshapes meant.

How would you ask for a glass of water if you didn't know that the wet stuff you drink and the hard container you put it in have names? Helen says her soul woke up the day she realized that everything had a name. It happened like this. One morning while she was washing, Helen pointed to the water and patted her teacher's hand. Anne spelled W-A-T-E-R into her hand. Later that day they went out to the pump. Helen held her mug under the spout while Anne pumped the water.

When the mug filled up, the water gushed over Helen's hand. Anne fingerspelled W-A-T-E-R into Helen's other hand — and suddenly Helen understood. W-A-T-E-R meant the wet cold something she could feel on her hand. Because Helen Keller couldn't see or hear, her hands were the life-line that connected her to her world, and Anne Sullivan fingerspelled that whole world into her hands.

Later in her life, Helen Keller said:
"I have met people so empty of joy, that when I clasped their frosty fingertips, it seemed as if I were shaking hands with a northeast storm. Others there are whose hands have sunbeams in them, so that their grasp warms my heart."

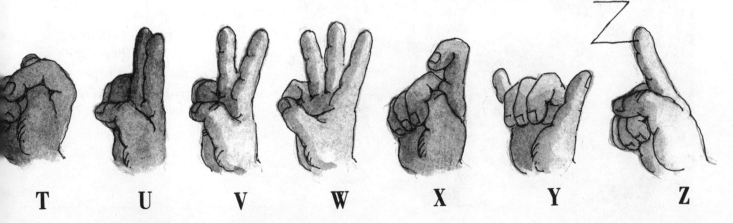

T   U   V   W   X   Y   Z

DEXTER AND FRIEND

Helen Keller could talk only to people who understood fingerspelling. Today, she could have a conversation with anyone with the help of Dexter, a robot hand, and its friend, a talking glove.

Dexter (the name comes from the Latin for right hand) is a robot hand that can make all 26 letters in the fingerspelled alphabet.

When you type words onto a computer keyboard, Dexter fingerspells them for the deaf-and-blind person. Dexter whips along at two letters a second, but that's still slower than a human hand.

The talking glove works the other way; it translates fingerspelling into spoken words. As the user fingerspells the words, sensors in the back of the glove read the handshapes. The fingerspelled words go to a mini-computer attached to the person's belt, where the words are changed into speech. Then the spoken words come out of a little speaker hanging around the person's neck.

Today, computers and robots are helping to break down the walls that separate the deaf and the deaf-and-blind from the world around them.

FRIENDLY NAME SIGNS

You always fingerspell a person's name when you first introduce her. But fingerspelling takes a long time, and there may be several Cathys or Toms in a group. So people have sign language symbols called Name Signs.

Name Signs are usually made with the handshape of the first letter of the name, and tell the watcher something about the person. If someone named Lee always wears a very big watch, her name sign might be the L handshape made on the wrist, where she wears her watch. To describe a policeman named Bob, you might make the B handshape on your chest to show his badge.

EVERYONE SPOKE SIGN

Martha's Vineyard is the largest island off the coast of New England. It was first settled by Europeans in 1644, but by 1710 all the good land was taken and immigration stopped. People did not leave the island, and very few new people arrived, so most of the Islanders were descendants of the first settlers.

Because some of those first families carried a gene for deafness, many deaf people were born on the island. So everybody, both hearing and deaf, spoke a special Island sign language that gradually developed over the years.

When fishermen and farmers gathered at the general store, the conversation was in spoken language and sign—sometimes both at the same time. Fishermen in their boats on the open water would raise their hands high above their heads so they could be seen and tell each other how many lobsters they had caught. Women at home during the day could talk to a friend on a neighbouring farm using sign language—and a spyglass. People who could hear got so used to using sign language that they used it when it was difficult to talk— or when they weren't supposed to!

Children learned sign language the way they learned to speak, because it was being used around them all the time—in their families, at church, in school. They could tell a teacher they weren't talking in class, then they could go on "talking" in sign language. This worked only if the teacher had come from "off-Island" and didn't know about Island sign!

Today, on Martha's Vineyard, only the elderly people remember sign language. Nora Groce, an anthropologist who studied deafness on the Island, asked a woman about people she knew who were handicapped by deafness. The women said that those people weren't handicapped. They were just deaf.

Signs from the past

Sign language has a very long history. In ancient Greece, people who were deaf and couldn't talk communicated using signs.

The first people who wrote down lists of signs were monks. They were speaking sign language nearly a thousand years ago. In some religious orders, the monks promised not to speak in certain places and at certain times. The chapel and the refectory where they ate were places where they "talked" using only signs. These early signs had to do with everyday life in the monastery. There were signs for different kinds of bread, fish, vegetables and fruits and also signs for all the things needed to celebrate mass.

Today, Cistercian monks still use sign language. Some of the signs are the traditional ones, but new ones are always being invented, just the way new words are added to a spoken language. Modern monks needed a sign for tractor, a machine that didn't exist in the Middle Ages. The modern Cistercians combined the sign for **red** and the sign for **horse**.

Bulldozer is **bull** + **push**.

Many Cistercian signs are strings of hand gestures. Star is **little** + **night** + **time** + **light**. Then you point up.

Here are some Cistercian signs that are clever and funny: "Oh dear"—Sign **O** + **deer**. For pumpernickel (that's a kind of bread)—Sign **pump** + **r** + **five** + **cents**. Get it? Five cents is a nickel.

Charles Michel de l'Epée was a French abbé who opened a school for deaf children in Paris in 1760. For the first time ever, deaf children who were not rich could come to school. L'Epée's school was important because it brought together many deaf people in one place. It created a deaf community.

L'Epée noticed that many of the deaf children, especially those who had deaf parents, communicated using signs. When these deaf people "talked" to each other, they didn't fingerspell the French words. They skipped spoken language.

L'Epée combined these "natural signs" with some Cistercian signs. He also added grammar signs—signs for verb tenses and singular and plural—to make the language more like spoken French.

Abbé Sicard, who continued L'Epée's work, stopped using the grammar signs. He taught his pupils the French words for things, and they taught him the signs that they used. So together, deaf students and their teachers created the language of signs.

Thomas Gallaudet brought this sign language to the United States. The French signs and the natural signs used by the American deaf community were the roots of American Sign Language.

IN CHINA . . .

In China, people speak many different dialects, but they can communicate using signs. The signs they use are the characters of the written language, which are the same for everyone. So someone who speaks Mandarin can talk to someone who speaks Cantonese by drawing the written character in the air or on the palm of her hand.

Indian sign language –

The sign talk of the Plains Indians has been called the first American language. The Plains Indians were buffalo hunters who lived on the great plains, or prairies, of North America. Many different tribes, each with its own language, shared this huge area. When they needed to communicate with each other, to trade or make treaties, they used signs that everybody understood. Indian Sign Language was an old and poetic way of speaking. It was a safe way of speaking too, because people could talk to each other just outside of arrow range!

Expert sign talkers used flowing, curved movements.

They signed with calm expressions on their faces, using only the signs to carry the message. The signs were nearly all picture-like, so the language was easy to learn and understand.

Ernest Thompson Seton first saw this sign language in Manitoba. His book, *Sign Talk*, contains 1725 signs, most of them from the Cheyenne Indians, who were excellent signers. Thompson Seton hoped the sign language in his book would become an international language so that people all over the world could talk to each other.

In Indian Sign Language, thinking and understanding involve the heart, not the mind. The heart is the place where the intellect and the emotions live. Here is the sign for **heart**.

When you are **happy**, you have sunshine in your heart. So sign **heart**, then add the sign for **day**, the time when the sun shines. When you are **sad**, your heart is down on the ground. Sign **heart**, then take that **heart**

the language of the plains

sign, turn it over, open up your hand and drop it down towards the ground.

If you are **afraid**, your heart shakes. Make the sign for **heart**, and shake your hand up and down to show how your heart is jumping around inside. Or you can sign **heart**, then lift your hand up until the back hits under your chin. You're so scared, your heart is up in your throat!

When you **know** something, it's in your heart too. Use the L-shaped hand over your heart. Your hand curves out, then down. Turn the palm up. And when you **think**, the thought comes from your heart. This sign uses a G handshape over your heart, then moves it out and up.

When you're not sure about something, your heart is looking in two directions. To sign **maybe** or **perhaps**, make a V handshape. Put it over your heart with the back facing up. Then move your hand away from your chest in a little arc, until the back is facing out. If you are really in a dilemma, and don't know what to do, make the sign with five fingers spread out wide to show how many doubts you have.

A star is a sun that shines at night. The sign for **star** is **night + sun**. To show the star twinkling, you add the sign for **a little talk**. A star's twinkle is its **little star talk**.

The sign for **beaver** shows the beaver's tail hitting the mud or water. A **mouse** is a little **animal** that **nibbles** at **night**. A little night nibbler!

93

Mime

Mimes are performing artists who use their hands and bodies to tell stories without words. They and their audiences use their imaginations and together they create a make-believe world. We reach out with our hands and touch the world around us. A mime reaches out with her hands and makes a world exist. When she picks up a glass to take a drink, you see the glass even though it's not really there. The mime shapes the glass out of empty space using her hand. She knows how a hand looks when it is holding a glass and how the glass feels in her hand—and so do you.

Of course, a mime has to remember to put the glass down—unless she plans to let it crash to the floor. Once she's put it down she has to remember where it is. Her audience will notice if she lets her hand drift through the glass. And if she picks it up from a different spot, everyone will think it's a different glass! Mimes also have to remember to let go of the doorknobs on their imaginary doors and walk around, instead of through, imaginary tables.

If you want to be a mime, you have to learn how to handle space instead of objects. First, get your tools ready. Mimes do exercises to make their hands and fingers flexible. Since you're going to try some mime with your hands, warm up with these exercises.

Open and close your hands a few times. Now hold your hand in front of you, with the fingers pointing up as if you were saying "Stop." Start with your index finger and curl your fingers one by one down into the palm of your hand. Try to move each finger separately. Next, uncurl your fingers one at a time, starting with the little finger.

Try it again, but this time, curl down your little finger first and let the other fingers follow along. Now uncurl your fingers, starting with your index finger.

When you've done all this with one hand, exercise the other. You can also practise moving each finger around, one at a time.

Here's one more exercise: Shake your hands in the air to relax them. Now freeze your hands with your fingers spread out. When you freeze your hands, there's tension in them.

Do it again. Shake and freeze. Remember how your hand feels when it is relaxed, and remember how it feels when you freeze the movement.

Now you're ready to do some mime.

94

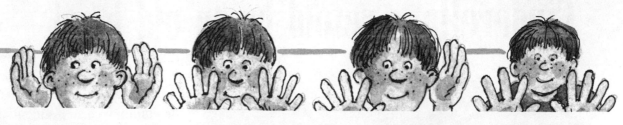

The wall

Put your hand on the back of your head. Feel the cup shape of your hand as it sits on your head. Take your hand off your head. Your hand is relaxed but it keeps its cup shape. Shape your other hand this way.

Hold your hands out in front of you. Imagine that there is a wall there. Put your hands on this wall. Spread your fingers wide so that your hands are flat. Freeze your hands.

Take your hands off the wall one at a time. Your hands go back into the cup shape when they're off the wall.

Put your hands back on the wall. Don't let your hands tip forwards or backwards. If they do, your wall will slant—and maybe fall over on you!

Now you know where your wall is. Where your hand and the wall meet should be a fixed point in space. Try moving your feet a few steps without moving your hands. How fixed is your fixed point?

Explore your wall to see how wide and how high it is. When you find the top, bend your fingers over it, as if you are holding on to the top edge of the wall. You can peep over the wall —stand on tiptoe if you like— but be careful not to pull the wall down as you pull yourself up to see over.

The table

Once you have created a flat surface like a wall, it's easy to make a table. A table is just a wall lying on its side.

Now imagine that there are some things lying on the table. Maybe a glass, a flower, a ball and anything else you like.

Pick up the glass. Keep your hand open as it moves towards the glass, then curl your fingers around it to create the shape. How does the glass feel? Take a drink. How does it taste? Don't forget to put the glass down.

Pick up the flower, gently. Use your thumb and index finger to hold it. How does it smell? Try doing "She loves me, she loves me not." Pull off each petal, look at it, let it drop. You might even watch it fall. Remember to put down the stem or throw it away.

Pick up the ball. Your hand is in its cup shape, but it's not relaxed this time, because it's holding something. Throw the ball up into the air. As the ball leaves your hand, it freezes flat. Watch the ball as it goes up and starts to come back down again. As you catch it, your hand goes back into its cup shape. Drop your hand a bit as it receives the weight of the ball. You can catch it every single time, or watch it bounce away.

Try passing some of the things on your table to a friend. Give away the flower, throw the ball and see what your friend's imagination does with the objects you've shaped.

Your hands can learn how to pick up and handle things that aren't there—to create them out of thin air—and make them so real that your audience will join you in your make-believe.

Cinderella - retold by an old hand

There are lots of hand words and phrases in the English language. See how many you can find in this strange retelling of a story that was written by Charles Perrault in the late 1600s and has been "handed down." Turn the page and use the handex to look up expressions you don't understand.

Once upon a time, there was a gentleman who gave his hand in marriage to a second wife. This second wife had her hands full with two spoilt daughters. They spent all their time admiring themselves in hand mirrors and never lent a helping hand around the house, although time often hung heavy on their hands. This gentleman had a daughter by his first marriage. She was beautiful and sweet tempered.

After the marriage, the second wife showed her true hand. She knew that in any contest of beauty and charm, her husband's daughter would beat her daughters hands down, so she made her do all the housework single-handed. This poor girl spent hours with her hands on the handle of a broom. She worked her fingers to the bone scrubbing floors and putting up shelves. Fortunately, she was very handy around the house.

She wore hand-me-down clothes and ate handouts from the table. She lived hand to mouth, but she was afraid to complain to her father because his new wife had the upper hand. When she had finished all the tasks at hand, she would go to the chimney corner and sit among the ashes — and so she was called Cinderella.

Now the king's son, who had a handsome handle-bar moustache, was giving a ball, and Cinderella's sisters were invited to be on hand. They were given a free hand with their father's money to purchase gowns, petticoats and lace-trimmed handkerchiefs for the ball. Cinderella had more work to do than ever, for her sisters expected to be waited on hand and foot. They kept flying off the handle everytime something was less than perfect. Nevertheless, Cinderella had a hand in everything, for her sisters knew she had good ideas, and they were both ham-handed.

At last the day of the ball was at hand. Cinderella watched her sisters ride off to court, feeling second-hand. But fortunately, Cinderella had a fairy godmother, who took her by the hand and said, "A little of my handiwork will make it possible for you to be on hand at the ball too." Cinderella was a bit sceptical, but she decided not to bite the hand that fed her, and that one bird in the hand — a chance to go to the ball — was better than two in the bush, so she did everything the fairy godmother asked. She handed over a pumpkin, six mice, a rat and six lizards. She threw up her hands in amazement when she saw her godmother — an old hand at magic — turn them into a golden coach, six horses and a coachman and six footmen. Her hand-me-down rags were handily transformed into a beautiful gown, and on her feet were glass slippers.

"The magic ends at twelve midnight," warned the fairy godmother. "I wash my hands of anything that happens after that."

"Don't worry. I promise to be home by midnight," said Cinderella. "It's out of your hands now."

Cinderella and the handsome prince danced hand in hand all evening. They danced together with such ease and grace that the guests gave them a hand at the end of each waltz. Cinderella's sisters, on the other hand, didn't dance at all. As the hands of the clock reached twelve midnight, Cinderella remembered the promise she had given to her fairy godmother. She shook hands with the prince, then, without telling him her name, she fled from the ball. She was in such a hurry that she lost one of her glass slippers.

Soon after this, a letter was sent by hand to all the households of the kingdom. The prince wanted the hand of the beautiful princess whose foot would fit the glass slipper. He handed over the glass slipper and the job of finding the princess to his servant—his right-hand man.

"Hands off," said Cinderella's sisters, when she asked to try on the slipper. But the servant had orders to let everyone try her hand at making the slipper fit.

When the sisters realized that the slipper was Cinderella's, they saw the handwriting on the wall and begged her pardon for the offhand way they had treated her. Cinderella acted handsomely and forgave them all the injustices she had suffered at their hands.

The servant led Cinderella to the prince, who, cap in hand, asked for her hand in marriage. They were married and lived happily like hand and glove forever after.

Handex

When **time hangs heavy on your hands** you have nothing to do, and time is passing slowly.

When you **show your hand**, you're letting the other players in a card game know what you're really up to. Cinderella's stepmother was showing her true personality.

When a jockey wins a race **hands down**, he's winning easily. Because he's so far ahead, he's riding with his hands resting down on the horse's neck, letting the horse finish the race at its own speed.

A **handle**, of course, is the part of something you take or hold with your hand.

When you live **hand to mouth**, you're not thinking about tomorrow. You eat all the food you have, without putting any aside. It wasn't poor Cinderella's fault that she had to live hand to mouth, though.

If you have the **upper hand** in a situation, you have the advantage.

A **handle-bar moustache** is usually large and it's shaped like . . . guess what? A handle-bar, of course.

If you have a **free hand** with something, it means you can do what you want, without asking anyone else's opinion. Some kids have a free hand with their allowance.

When you wait on someone **hand and foot**, you're her slave. If a person **flies off the handle**, he's lost his temper—or his head—just the way an axe head might dangerously fly off its handle.

If you're **ham-handed**, you're pretty clumsy and bungling. Can you imagine what it would be like to have two hams dangling at the end of your arms? Cinderella was smart when she decided not to **bite the hand that fed her**. If you're nasty to someone who's doing you a good turn, he won't help you again.

When the guests **gave** Cinderella and the prince **a hand**, they actually put two hands together for them—they clapped.

When you **wash your hands of something**, you won't take any more responsibility for what happens. This expression refers to Pontius Pilate's action when he washed his hands at the trial of Jesus.

If a person is your **right-hand man**, he's useful and important to you—as useful and important as your right hand. If you're a leftie, you might want to call someone your **left-hand man**—or **woman**!

In the story of Daniel and the lion's den, Daniel explains the mysterious **handwriting on the wall** of the palace during a great feast. The words warn the king, Belshazzar, that his rule is about to end, and his kingdom will be divided. So writing on the wall is a warning.

When you treat someone in an **offhand** way, you're casual, curt or rude.

The Prince and Cinderella lived like **hand and glove**—that means they went well together and they were as close as a hand and a glove are.

MENE, MENE, EKEL, UP-HARSIN.

The last word on handtalk

Shaking twice

It's considered bad luck to shake hands with someone twice. To undo the bad luck, quickly shake hands with that friend a third time.

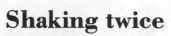

The talking hand

This old trick lets you practise ventriloquism anytime, anywhere.

To turn your hand into a face, make a fist. Now draw eyes and a nose on your index finger and a curved chin line on your thumb.

You make the mouth open by rolling your thumb down, away from your index finger. Close the mouth by rolling your thumb back up to meet your index finger again.

You can add hair, a moustache, or even a bow tie to your talking hand.

THE WACKY WAVE

Here's how to turn your real hand into a mechanical one that waves up and down when you pull on an imaginary thread.

Pretend to sew your fingers together. Start by threading an imaginary needle. You'll need a long piece of imaginary thread. Hold your imaginary needle in one hand. Spread out the fingers of your other hand. The imaginary needle goes into one side of your little finger and comes out the other side. Pull the needle out and show your audience how long the thread is. The imaginary needle goes through your ring finger next. The thread pulls your little finger and ring finger

together. One at a time, sew your middle finger and index finger to the others. Add your thumb. The imaginary thread holds it against the side of your index finger.

To make your waving apparatus go up and down, sew the imaginary thread through your wrist, from the back to the front, then through your elbow. The thread is hanging out below your elbow. Now pull on the thread and make your hand flap up and down.

Prints

You probably already know how to make a thumbprint and a basic Thumb-one—two eyes, a nose and a mouth—but here are some Thumb-things and Thumb-people to spark your imagination.

Paints dabbed onto a damp paper towel work like a stamp pad. Or you can use a real stamp pad if you don't mind walking around for several days with multi-coloured fingers.

When you start to print, use your fingers as well as your thumb. And experiment with the prints of different parts of your hand. The bottom part of your palm, called the "heel" of your hand, can make the body of a seal or one wing of a butterfly.

The side of your hand from the wrist up to the tip of your little finger makes a great bird; for the body and trunk of an elephant, just add legs.

Combine different hand, finger and thumbprints in one picture. You'll be amazed at the shapes you find when you start to print parts of your hand.

BIRDMAN MASK

Use your hands to make a pair of aviator goggles, like the ones worn by early pilots or "birdmen."

Put the tips of your right index finger and thumb together. Put the tips of your left index finger and thumb together. Now put your index fingers and thumbs together to make the goggles.

There's only one problem. Your goggles are upside-down. You have to turn them right-side-up as you bring them up to your eyes.

If you're feeling silly, flap your elbows in the air and fly around the house saying:

Up in the air, Junior Birdmen,
Up in the air upside down.
Up in the air, Junior Birdmen,
Keep your elbows off the ground.
When your hear the doorbells ringing,
When you see the wings of tin,
Then you'll know the Junior Birdmen
Have sent their boxtops in.
It takes five boxtops, four labels, three coupons,
two bottlecaps and one thin di-i-ime.

Oh my goodness, oh my soul,
Here comes the Junior Bird patrol.

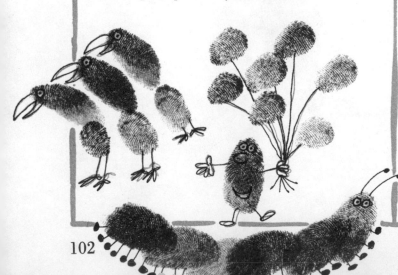

Trace your hand and . . .

Thirty thousand years ago, early people made prints and stencils of their hands on the walls of caves in Spain and France. They outlined the hand by blowing coloured pigment around the edges with a blowpipe. Their handprints and stencils were signatures that said, "We were here."

There are lots of hands in North American Indian rock art, too. The hands are carved or painted in the rock, and they're often decorated with zigzag or spiral patterns. Some hands even have fingerprints.

Trace your hand or make a wet handprint on the sidewalk. Draw around the handprint with chalk. Now decorate the hand, or turn it into something else. Here are some ideas.

- Draw a self-portrait. Don't forget your braids, curls or baseball cap.

- Make a monster. Your monster can have five legs or five heads. Fringe it, polka-dot or spot it, or make it green and lumpy with pimples!

- Make a beast of your hand. Draw around your hand, but try putting different fingers together as you trace them.

- Make a snake, or a whole snake family. Try a lion or a floppy-eared dog. Your dog can bark or be quiet. Move your thumb to open and close his mouth.

- Create a world of hands. You can make birds and butterflies, leaves on a tree or on a Christmas wreath. Just use your imagination.

Shadows on the wall

Did you ever sit up in bed at night and see a dark shadowy monster on the wall of your room? How long did it take before you realized it was the shadow of your jacket hanging on your bedpost? Shadows of objects look a lot different than the objects themselves. That's why you can turn your two hands into a bird, a rabbit or an elephant's head.

There are some things you should know before you start playing with shadows. A smaller light source is better than a larger light source. Try a reading lamp. Make sure it has a clear glass light bulb. (The frosty kind are for people who don't want shadows.) A flashlight will give you even clearer shadow pictures than a lamp. When your hands stop all the light falling on them, they cast a dark shadow called an umbra. When some of the light gets past your hands and shines on their shadow, it makes it lighter. The lighter shadow is called the penumbra. The penumbra fuzzes up the outline of your shadow hands.

For a screen, you can tape a piece of white paper to a wall, or you can use a bare wall that's a light colour.

You need to sit or stand in between the light source and the wall, so that the light source, you and the screen are in a straight line. Move the light source or move closer to the wall until your get dark shadows with clear outlines. Don't watch your hands. Watch the shadows. Try making some of these shadow pictures—they're from the *Boys' Own Annual* for 1879.

SHADOWS

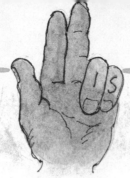

This is your face

Make a fist. Write THIS on your fingers. Make sure the word reads the right way for the person looking at you.
Write YOUR on your fingers near where you wear your rings.

Open out your hand, and draw a funny little face on your palm.
Make long hairs going up your fingers.
Now find a friend.
Make a fist to show the THIS.
"This. . ."
Lift up two fingers to leave IS.
". . . is . . ."

Make a fist again. Tip your hand to show the YOUR.
". . . your . . ." Open out your hand to show the face. Pop your hand forward towards your friend. ". . . face!"

Walking wonders

Let your fingers do the walking with these finger puppets.

If you're making a person puppet, use an index card the tall way. Turn the card on its side to draw an animal. Don't draw the legs. Of course, if you're making an octopus, you have to draw three legs—your fingers will be the other five.

To make holes big enough for your fingers, draw around a dime. Cut the circles out.

Make a lion, a person, or the world's first dancing snowman. If you like, you can cut out little boots for the snowman and stick them to your fingernails with tape—after all, it's probably too cold for bare feet. If the boots keep falling off, tape them to rings of paper that you can wear around the tips of your fingers.

Now let your walking wonders jump, dance, march—or swim.

The finger frog

You're off to catch a frog.

First, make a trap. Start with your hands palms up. Cross your little fingers over each other. Then cross your ring fingers over each other. These four fingers are the sticks that make the frog trap.

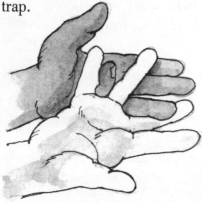

To set the trap, hook your right middle finger down over your left ring finger. Your left middle finger hooks down over your right ring finger.

To start making the frog, slide your index fingers under your ring fingers. Your ring fingers are poking out between your middle and index fingers. They're the eyes of the frog.

To make the frog's mouth, swing your left thumb around to meet your left index finger, pad to pad. Your right thumb swings around to meet your right index finger. Index fingers and thumbs come together in the centre to

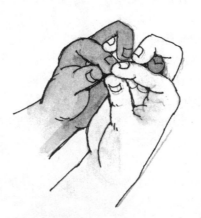

make the mouth. Open and close the mouth by separating your index fingers from your thumbs, and bringing them back together.

You can make a wolf that looks a bit like the frog, but he's made a different way to give him a longer nose.

Start with your hands palms up. Put your hands together so that your little fingers are side by side. Your little fingers are the wolf's ears.

To start making the wolf's face, tip down your middle fingers. The sides of your middle fingertips are touching. Tip down your right ring finger. It rests on the

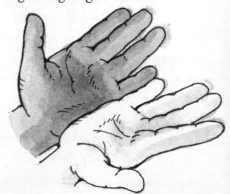

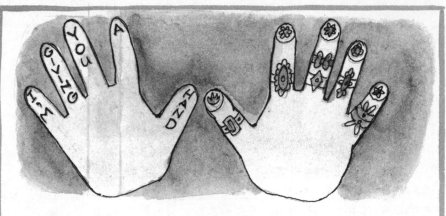

back of your left middle finger. Tip down your left ring finger. It crosses over your right ring finger and rests on the back of your right middle finger.

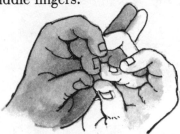

To make the wolf's eyes, hook your right index finger up over your left ring finger and hook your left index finger up over your right ring finger. The eyes of the wolf—your ring fingers—are sticking out between your index fingers and middle fingers.

To make the wolf's mouth, swing your thumbs around towards the front. They meet each other and the pads of your middle fingers.

Open the mouth by separating your thumbs from your middle fingers. Close the mouth by bringing them back together.

Give someone a hand

When you give someone a hand, you're saying, "Bravo." Give someone you like a hand today.

Draw around your hand and cut it out.

Write I'M GIVING YOU A HAND on the fingers and thumb, or put another message there.

When you've finished decorating and writing on one side, turn the hand over. Add fancy fingernails or rings and the person's name.

Fold down the fingers to close up the card, little finger first, thumb last, and put on a tiny piece of tape to keep the card shut. Now hand-deliver it or put it in an envelope to mail it.

Tell a story

Turn your fingertips into Goldilocks and the three bears, kings and queens, princes and princesses.

You need markers to draw on faces, and coloured paper for ears or crowns. Use wool for hair and fabric or ribbon scraps for costumes. White glue or tape holds it all together.

With a few friends you can make a cast of thousands—well, almost.

The best clapping game

Here's a clapping game that's fun to do with a friend. It has ten steps, so it takes a little while to learn, but it's worth the effort.

You and your friend each put your hands together palm to palm. Your fingers are pointing away from you.

You and your friend put your pairs of hands back to back. Four hands are lined up in a row. Your hands are pointing one way, your friend's hands are pointing the other way. You each have a back-to-back hand and a free hand.

Now you're ready to start the clap.

1. Your free hands clap your back-to-back hands. "Clap."

2. Move your free hands up to clap each other. "Clap Up."

3. Your free hands clap your back-to-back hands again. "Clap."

4. Your free hands move down and around to grab each other. Hold on. "Grab."

5. Your back-to-back hands move down and around to grab each other. Hold on. You hold on all the way to Step 10. "Grab."

6. The free hands that first grabbed each other let go and slap your legs. "Slap."

7. The free hands snap their fingers. "Snap."

8. The free hands slap fronts. "Slap Fronts."

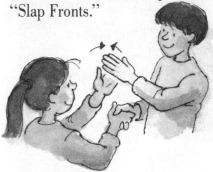

9. The free hands slap backs and stay there. "Slap Backs."

10. Your free hands are now the back-to-back hands. You're ready to start again. Let go of each other's hands. The ones that were holding on are the free hands now. Bring them up to clap the back-to-back hands.

The clap has changed sides, so this time you slap the other leg and snap the fingers of your other hand.

This clap works well with "See, see my playmate." Try it with the words of other clapping games you know.

Bibliography

I would like to take this opportunity to acknowledge some of the many reference works I consulted during the preparation of this book.

Backhouse, Kenneth; Hutchings, Ralph T. *Color Atlas of Surface Anatomy*. Baltimore: Williams and Williams, 1986.

Duponchel, Laurent; Lafage, Suzanne. *Murmures des Lagunes et des Savanes*. Paris: Conseil International de la Langue Francaise: EDICEF, 1975.

Herzog, George. *Jabo Proverbs from Liberia*. London: Oxford University Press, 1936.

Klima, Edward; Bellugi, Ursula. *The Signs of Language*. Cambridge, MA.: Harvard University Press, 1979.

Lambert, David. *The Cambridge Guide to Prehistoric Man*. Cambridge: Cambridge University Press, 1987.

Leakey, Richard E.; Lewin, Roger. *Origins*. New York: E.P. Dutton, 1977.

Morris, Desmond. *Gestures: their origins and distribution*. London: Jonathan Cape, 1979.

——————. *Manwatching: a field guide to human behaviour*. London: Jonathan Cape, 1977.

Napier, John Russell. *Hands*. London: Allen and Unwin, 1980.

Neisser, Arden. *The Other Side of Silence*. New York: Knopf, 1983.

Opie, Iona and Peter. *The Lore and Language of Schoolchildren*. Oxford: Oxford University Press, 1959.

Riekehof, Lottie L. *The Joy of Signing*. Springfield, MO: Gospel Publishing House, 1978.

Seton, Ernest Thompson. *Sign Talk*. Garden City, NY: Doubleday, Page and Company, 1918.

Springer, Sally P.; Deutsch, Georg. *Left Brain, Right Brain*. New York: W.H. Freeman and Co., 1989.

PERMISSIONS AND PHOTO CREDITS

Page 5: Excerpt from "Learning From the Hands" © 1985 by Bronwen Wallace, published in *Common Magic*. Used by permission of the publisher, Oberon Press.

Pages 23 and 72: Cartoons by Gary Larson are reprinted by permission of *Chronicle Features*, San Francisco.

Page 24: Illustration of General Tom Thumb from *A Sketch of the Life, Personal Appearance, Character and Manners of Charles S. Stratton, the Man in Miniature, Known as General Tom Thumb*, Press of Wynkoop and Hallenbeck, 1869. Reproduced from the collection of the Thomas Fisher Rare Book Library, University of Toronto.

Pages 58 and 66: "Pinkety, Pinkety" and "Salute the Captain of the Ship" from *The Lore and Language of Schoolchildren* © 1959 by Iona and Peter Opie. Used by permission of the publisher, Oxford University Press.

Page 69: Courtesy of NASA.

Page 88: Courtesy of Stanford News Service.

Page 104: Illustrations from *The Boy's Own Paper*, 1879. Reprinted from the Osborne Collection of Early Children's Books, Toronto Public Library.

Index

	DATE DUE		